Lord Hear Our Prayer

Prayer is the light of the soul, giving us true knowledge of God. Prayer is a precious way of communicating with God, it gladdens the soul and gives repose to its affections.

St. John Chrysostom

Lord Hear Our Prayer

compiled by

Thomas McNally, C.S.C.

and

William G. Storey, D.M.S.

AVE MARIA PRESS
Notre Dame, Indiana 46556

Nihil Obstat: David Burrell, C.S.C.
            Censor Deputatus
Imprimatur: William E. McManus
            Bishop of Fort Wayne-South Bend

First printing, October, 1978
Fifth printing, October, 1987
90,000 copies in print

Library of Congress Catalog Card Number: 78-67423
International Standard Book Number: 0-87793-163-1

© 1978 by Ave Maria Press, Notre Dame, Indiana 46556
Art by Janet Trzaska
Printed and bound in the United States of America.

ACKNOWLEDGMENTS:

American Bible Society. *The Good News Bible*. © American Bible Society 1966, 1971, 1976. Unless otherwise indicated, all scripturual passages are from *The Good News Bible*. Reprinted by permission.

Cambridge University Press. *The New English Bible*. © 1970.The delegates of the Oxford University Press and the Syndics of the Cambridge University Press 1961, 1970. For six short New Testament passages. Reprinted by permission.

Confraternity of Christian Doctrine, Inc. *The New American Bible*. © 1970. For a number of passages from the Psalms and New Testament.

International Committee on English in the Liturgy, Inc. For excerpts from the English translation of the Roman Missal © 1973; excerpts from Morning Prayer, Evening Prayer, and Office of Readings from the *Liturgy of the Hours* (c) 1974; and two prayers from the English translation of the *Rite of Penance* © 1974, 1975. All rights reserved.

International Consultation on English Texts. *Prayers We Have In Common*. © 1975. For the "Lord's Prayer," the "Apostles' Creed," "Gloria Patri," "Benedictus," "Te Deum," "Magnificat," and "Nunc Dimittis."

World Library Publications. *Biblical Prayers* by Lucien Deiss. © 1976, Lucien Deiss. All rights reserved. For ten prayers: "Make Your Light Shine," "For People of All Ages," "For the Church of Your Son, Jesus," "The Good Shepherd," "Like Children," "God of Our Childhood," "I Have Spent My Life, Lord," "Stay With Us, Lord," "Come to Me Like a Cry of Joy," and "Your Spirit, Lord, Is Truth." With permission.

(Additional acknowledgments on pp. 358–360)

Contents

Preface

IT'S NO SECRET that we live in a frantic age; and the pace seems to quicken day by day instead of slowing down. Some psychologists are wondering if human beings can accept and absorb all the changes that our technological society calls on us to make. How much can we take before we fly to pieces?

That's why it's so important for us at times to "idle down," to put the brakes on activity. Wise men and women, whether believers or not, recognize this fact and find time for stillness and reflection in various ways.

And we who believe in the loving Father, and the Son he sent and the promise of the Holy Spirit, see a need not simply for stillness but for prayer. After all, our lives are not our own but God's, and prayer is our fumbling attempt to affirm this.

11

By that I don't mean to imply that prayer is simply a problem-solving device, a selfish way to make our lives more bearable. Above all, it is our way to praise and thank the Father for all he is and all he has done.

Furthermore, as Thomas Merton suggests, we are not talking here about simply a private enterprise. Silence, solitude and prayer are not private projects, says Merton, but belong to the people with whom we live and work. Not only that, but through faith, my prayer puts me in touch with all those millions whom I shall never meet but for whom I pray daily, including those ravaged by poverty, grief and injustice.

In some mysterious way my prayer today is not simply "mine" but belongs to the whole community; and I am comforted by the knowledge that your prayer has room in it for me! There's an expression in Latin—*Oremus pro invicem*—which says it all: Let us pray for each other!

Because of the tremendous importance of prayer in our day, I'm delighted to see this book emanate from the University of Notre Dame. In the '60s and early '70s new prayer-books were hardly in large supply. There were many reasons for this, including the inevitable uncertainties and changes following the great Second Vatican Council.

My hope, and the hope of the editors and publishers, is that this book will help put prayer in focus again for thousands of Christians; and that it will put them back in touch with the rich Christian tradition of prayer. Furthermore, our hope is that the book will help move Christians forward in their prayer life, because prayer is not static but dynamic and cannot be limited to a particular style or time.

The Lord put it best: "Out of his storehouse, the home-owner brought forth things both new and old" (Mt 13:52). The editors have reached into that storehouse and rummaged around for the best in prayers both old and new. I think they have succeeded remarkably well, and hope you will agree with me after sampling *Lord, Hear Our Prayer*.

Oremus pro invicem
Theodore M. Hesburgh, C.S.C.

Prayer is the means whereby we rightly
understand the fullness of joy that is
coming to us.

Julian of Norwich (1342–1416)

1. Everyday Prayers

Our parents and teachers inscribed some prayers on our memories when we were young, and we will never forget the words. (We have, however, included the modern version of the Lord's Prayer, in addition to the one we learned!)

Other prayers, like grace before and after meals, and acts of faith, hope, charity and contrition come in various versions.

In this section, we present these prayers which are common to most of us from our youth in one form or another.

The Lord's Prayer

Our Father, who art in heaven,
hallowed be thy Name;
thy kingdom come;
thy will be done on earth
   as it is in heaven.
Give us this day our daily bread;
and forgive us our trespasses
as we forgive those who trespass
   against us;
and lead us not into temptation,
but deliver us from evil.

For thine is the kingdom and the power
   and the glory for ever and ever.

The Lord's Prayer

(Modern Version)

Our Father in heaven,
   hallowed be your Name,
   your kingdom come,
   your will be done,
      on earth as in heaven.
Give us today our daily bread.
Forgive us our sins
   as we forgive those who sin against us.
Save us from the time of trial
   and deliver us from evil.

For the kingdom, the power and the glory are
      yours,
   now and for ever.

The Hail Mary

Hail, Mary, full of grace, the Lord is with
      you.
Blessed are you among women,
and blessed is the fruit of your womb, Jesus.
Holy Mary, Mother of God, pray for us
      sinners,
   now and at the hour of our death.   Amen.

The Apostles' Creed

I believe in God, the Father almighty,
  creator of heaven and earth.

I believe in Jesus Christ, his only son, our
  Lord.
  He was conceived by the power of the
    Holy Spirit
    and born of the Virgin Mary.
  He suffered under Pontius Pilate,
    was crucified, died, and was buried.
  He descended to the dead.
  On the third day he rose again.
  He ascended into heaven,
    and is seated at the right hand of the
    Father.
  He will come again to judge the living and
    the dead.
I believe in the Holy Spirit,
  the holy catholic Church,
  the communion of saints,
  the forgiveness of sins,
  the resurrection of the body,
  and the life everlasting.

The Doxology

Glory to the Father, and to the Son, and to
  the Holy Spirit:
as it was in the beginning, is now, and will
  be for ever.   Amen.

An Act of Faith

O God,
I firmly believe all the truths that you have
    revealed
and that you teach us through your Church,
for you are truth itself
and can neither deceive nor be deceived.

An Act of Hope

O God,
I hope with complete trust that you will
    give me,
through the merits of Jesus Christ,
all necessary grace in this world
and everlasting life in the world to come,
for this is what you have promised
and you always keep your promises.

An Act of Love

O God,
I love you with my whole heart
    above all things,
because you are infinitely good;
and for your sake I love my neighbor as I love
    myself.

An Act of Contrition

O God,
I am sorry with my whole heart for all my
    sins
because you are Goodness itself
and sin is an offense against you.
Therefore, I firmly resolve,
with the help of your grace,
not to sin again and to avoid the occasions
    of sin.

God, We Praise You

You are God: we praise you;
You are the Lord: we acclaim you;
You are the eternal Father:
All creation worships you.

To you all angels, all the powers of heaven,
Cherubim and Seraphim, sing in endless
    praise:
  Holy, holy, holy Lord, God of power and
    might,
  heaven and earth are full of your glory.

The glorious company of apostles praise you.
The noble fellowship of prophets praise you.
The white-robed army of martyrs praise you.

Throughout the world the holy Church
 acclaims you:
  Father, of majesty unbounded,
  your true and only Son, worthy of all
   worship,
  and the Holy Spirit, advocate and guide.

You, Christ, are the king of glory,
the eternal Son of the Father.
When you became man to set us free
you did not shun the Virgin's womb.

You overcame the sting of death
and opened the kingdom of heaven to all
 believers.
You are seated at God's right hand in glory.
We believe that you will come and be our
 judge.

  Come then, Lord, and help your people,
  bought with the price of your own blood,
  and bring us with your saints
  to glory everlasting.

Te Deum Laudamus

We are commanded to worship, not on
 special days, but continuously all our life
 through, and in all possible ways.
Clement of Alexandria

Glory to God

Glory to God in the highest,
  and peace to his people on earth.

Lord God, heavenly King,
almighty God and Father,
  we worship you, we give you thanks,
  we praise you for your glory.

Lord Jesus Christ, only Son of the Father,
Lord God, Lamb of God,
you take away the sin of the world:
  have mercy on us;
you are seated at the right hand of the Father:
  receive our prayer.

For you alone are the Holy One,
you alone are the Lord,
you alone are the Most High,
  Jesus Christ,
  with the Holy Spirit,
  in the glory of God the Father. Amen.

Gloria in Excelsis

Come, Holy Spirit

Come, Holy Spirit, fill the hearts of your
    faithful
  and kindle in them the fire of your love.

Send forth your Spirit, O Lord,
  and renew the face of the earth.

O God,
on the first Pentecost
you instructed the hearts of those who
    believed in you
by the light of the Holy Spirit:
under the inspiration of the same Spirit,
give us a taste for what is right and true
and a continuing sense of his joy-bringing
    presence and power,
through Jesus Christ our Lord.
—Amen.

The Angelus

The angel of the Lord brought the message to
    Mary.
  And she conceived of the Holy Spirit.
    Hail Mary . . .

I am the Lord's servant;
  May it happen to me as you have said.
    Hail Mary . . .

And the Word was made flesh;
  And dwelt among us.
    Hail Mary . . .

Pray for us, O holy Mother of God;
  that we may be made worthy of the
    promises of Christ.

Pour forth, O Lord,
your grace into our hearts,
that we to whom the incarnation of Christ
    your Son
was made known by the message of an
    angel,
may by his passion and cross be brought to
    the glory of his resurrection;
through the same Christ our Lord.
—Amen.

The Memorare

Remember, O most gracious Virgin Mary,
that never was it known that anyone who
    fled to your protection,
implored your help, or sought your
    intercession was left unaided.
Inspired by this confidence, we fly unto you,
O Virgin of virgins, our Mother!
To you we come, before you we stand, sinful
    and sorrowful.
O Mother of the Word incarnate,
despise not our petitions,
but in your mercy hear and answer us.
—Amen.

Grace Before Meals

All living things look to you
  to give them their food in due season.
You give it, they gather it up:
  you open your hand, they have their fill.
Glory to the Father, and to the Son, and to
    the Holy Spirit:
  as it was in the beginning, is now, and will
    be for ever.   Amen.

Bless us, O Lord, and these your gifts
which we are about to receive from your
    bounty,
through Christ our Lord.
—Amen.

Grace After Meals

Let all the works of the Lord bless the Lord,
   and his children shall praise him for ever.
Glory to the Father, and to the Son, and to
      the Holy Spirit:
   as it was in the beginning, is now, and will
      be for ever.   Amen.

We give you thanks, Almighty God,
for these and all your blessings;
you live and reign for ever and ever.
—Amen.

A Brief Morning Prayer

Hymn

Now that the daylight fills the sky
We lift our hearts to God on high,
That he, in all we do or say,
Would keep us free from harm today:

Would guard our hearts and tongues from
      strife,
From anger's din would hide our life,
From evil sights would turn our eyes,
Would close our ears to vanities.

So we, when this new day is gone
And night in turn is drawing on,
With conscience by the world unstained
Shall praise his name for victory gained.

To God the Father and the Son
And Holy Spirit, three in one,
Be endless glory as before
The world began, so evermore.

Prayer

Almighty Father,
you have brought us to the light of a new
     day:
keep us safe the whole day through
from every sinful inclination.
May all our thoughts, words and actions
aim at doing what is pleasing in your sight.
We ask this through Christ our Lord.
—Amen.

Blessing

May the Lord order our days and our deeds
     in his peace.
—Amen.

A Brief Night Prayer

Hymn

As twilight now draws near its close,
Creator of the world, we pray
That in your goodness you will be
Our stronghold till the coming day.

Grant rest without disturbing dreams.
Let nothing lead us into sin.
Ward off the evil one's assaults.
Bless, guard this night we now begin.

O loving Father, hear our prayer,
Through Christ your only Son our Lord:
One God, with God the Holy Ghost;
One King, eternally adored.

Prayer

Visit this house, O Lord, we pray,
and drive from it all snares of the enemy.
May your holy angels dwell here
    to keep us in peace,
and may your blessing be always upon us.
We ask this through Christ our Lord.
—Amen.

Blessing

May the Lord give us a peaceful night as
    day's perfect ending.
—Amen.

God is nearer to us than we are to ourselves.
St. Augustine

2. Prayers for All Seasons

MOST PRAYERS FLICKER briefly before the mind's eye and then vanish into darkness. But every age produces some prayers which find their way into print and survive because they touch the hearts of those who call themselves Christians.

Why do these prayers touch our hearts? Some are associated with great saints whose lives validate the words. But this is not the only reason. Whether written by saints long ago or men and women of our day, some prayers echo universal desires and sentiments.

Here, then, are prayers for all ages and all seasons.

29

Prayers from the Heart

Day by Day

Thank you, Lord Jesus Christ,
For all the benefits and blessings
   which you have given me,
For all the pains and insults
   which you have borne for me.
Merciful Friend, Brother and Redeemer,
May I know you more clearly,
Love you more dearly,
And follow you more nearly,
Day by day.

St. Richard of Chichester (1197–1253)

God Be in My Head

God be in my head
   and in my understanding.
God be in my eyes
   and in my looking.
God be in my mouth
   and in my speaking.
God be in my heart
   and in my thinking.
God be at my end
   and my departing.

Sarum Primer (1527)

invincible and keen:
We praise you, O Lord.

7. For our Mother Earth,
who sustains and feeds us,
producing fair fruits, many-colored
flowers and herbs:
We praise you, O Lord.

8. For those who forgive one another for
love of you,
and who patiently bear sickness and
other trials.
—Happy are they who peacefully
endure;
you will crown them, O Most High!—
We praise you, O Lord.

9. For our Sister Death,
the inescapable fact of life
—Woe to those who die in mortal sin!
Happy those she finds doing your
will!
From the Second Death they stand
immune—:
We praise you, O Lord.

10. All creatures,
praise and glorify my Lord
and give him thanks
and serve him in great humility.

WE PRAISE YOU, O LORD.

St. Francis of Assisi (1181–1226)
Trans. W.G.S.

Prayers for Light

A Spirit To Know You

Gracious and holy Father,
please give me:
intellect to understand you,
reason to discern you,
diligence to seek you,
wisdom to find you,
a spirit to know you,
a heart to meditate upon you,
ears to hear you,
eyes to see you,
a tongue to proclaim you,
a way of life pleasing to you,
patience to wait for you
and perseverance to look for you.
Grant me a perfect end—
your holy presence,
a blessed resurrection
and life everlasting.

Attributed to St. Benedict of Nursia (+555)

For Insight

May the Lord Jesus touch our eyes,
as he did those of the blind.
Then we shall begin to see
in visible things those which are invisible.
May he open our eyes to gaze,
not on present realities,
but on the blessings to come.
May he open the eyes of our heart
to contemplate God in Spirit,
through Jesus Christ the Lord, to whom
     belong
power and glory through all eternity.

Origen (185–253)

The Road Ahead

My Lord God,
I have no idea where I am going.
I do not see the road ahead of me.
I cannot know for certain where it will end.
Nor do I really know myself,
and the fact that I think that I am following
     your will does not mean
     that I am actually doing so.
But I believe that the desire to please you
     does in fact please you.
And I hope I have that desire in all that I am
     doing.
I hope that I will never do anything apart
     from that desire.

And I know that if I do this,
you will lead me by the right road though I
    may know nothing about it.
Therefore will I trust you always
though I may seem to be lost and in the
    shadow of death.
I will not fear, for you are ever with me,
and you will never leave me to face my perils
    alone.

Thomas Merton (1915–1968)

Flood the Path With Light

God of our life,
there are days when the burdens we carry
chafe our shoulders and weigh us down;
when the road seems dreary and endless,
the skies grey and threatening;
when our lives have no music in them,
and our hearts are lonely,
and our souls have lost their courage.
Flood the path with light,
turn our eyes to where the skies are full of
    promise;
tune our hearts to brave music;
give us the sense of comradeship
with heroes and saints of every age;
and so quicken our spirits
that we may be able to encourage
the souls of all who journey with us
on the road of life, to your honor and glory.

Attributed to St. Augustine (354–430)

Christ, Be With Me

Christ, be with me, Christ before me, Christ behind me,

Christ in me, Christ beneath me, Christ above me,

Christ on my right, Christ on my left,

Christ where I lie, Christ where I sit, Christ where I arise,

Christ in the heart of every one who thinks of me,

Christ in the mouth of every one who speaks of me,

Christ in every eye that sees me,

Christ in every ear that hears me.

Salvation is of the Lord.

Salvation is of the Lord,

Salvation is of the Christ.

May your salvation, O Lord, be ever with us.

St. Patrick's Breastplate (+461)

My Gift

Lord, I freely yield all my freedom to you.

Take my memory, my intellect and my entire will.

You have given me everything I am or have;

I give it all back to you to stand under your will alone.

Your love and your grace are enough for me;

I shall ask for nothing more.

St. Ignatius Loyola (1491–1556)

For Perfect Love

My God, I desire to love you perfectly,
With all my heart, which you made for
    yourself,
With all my mind, which you alone can
    satisfy,
With all my soul, which longs to soar to you,
With all my strength, my feeble strength
  which shrinks from so great a task
  and yet can choose nothing else
  but spend itself in loving you.
Claim my heart; free my mind;
Uplift my soul; reinforce my strength;
That where I fail, you may succeed in me
  and make me love you perfectly,
through Jesus Christ, my Lord.

Community of St. Mary the Virgin, Wantage

For a Magnanimous Heart

Keep us, O God, from all pettiness,
Let us be large in thought, in word, in deed.
Let us be done with faultfinding
  and leave off all self-seeking.
May we put away all pretense and meet each
    other face to face,
  without self-pity and without prejudice.
May we never be hasty in judgment,
  and always generous.
Let us always take time for all things,
  and make us grow calm, serene and gentle.

Teach us to put into action our better
impulses,
to be straightforward and unafraid.
Grant that we may realize
that it is the little things of life that create
differences,
that in the big things of life
we are as one.
And, O Lord God, let us not forget to be
kind!

Queen Mary Stuart (1542–1587)

For a Holy Heart

Lord, grant me a holy heart
that sees always what is fine and pure
and is not frightened at the sight of sin,
but creates order wherever it goes.
Grant me a heart that knows nothing
of boredom, weeping and sighing.
Let me not be too concerned
with the bothersome thing
I call "myself."
Lord, give me a sense of humor
and I will find happiness in life
and profit for others.

St. Thomas More (1478–1535)

Canticle of Brother Sun and Sister Moon

1. Most high, almighty, good Lord!
   All praise, glory, honor and exaltation
        are yours!
   To you alone do they belong,
   and no mere mortal dares pronounce
        your Name.

2. Praise to you, O Lord our God, for all
        your creatures:
   first, for our dear Brother Sun,
   who gives us the day
   and illumines us with his light;
   fair is he, in splendor radiant,
   bearing your very likeness, O Lord.

3. For our Sister Moon,
   and for the bright, shining stars:
   We praise you, O Lord.

4. For our Brother Wind,
   for fair and stormy seasons
   and all heaven's varied moods,
   by which you nourish all that you have
        made:
   We praise you, O Lord.

5. For our Sister Water,
   so useful, lowly, precious and pure:
   We praise you, O Lord.

6. For our Brother Fire,
   who brightens up our darkest nights:
   beautiful is he and eager,

invincible and keen:
We praise you, O Lord.

7. For our Mother Earth,
    who sustains and feeds us,
    producing fair fruits, many-colored
        flowers and herbs:
    We praise you, O Lord.

8. For those who forgive one another for
    love of you,
        and who patiently bear sickness and
            other trials.
    —Happy are they who peacefully
        endure;
        you will crown them, O Most High!—
        We praise you, O Lord.

9. For our Sister Death,
    the inescapable fact of life
    —Woe to those who die in mortal sin!
        Happy those she finds doing your
            will!
        From the Second Death they stand
            immune—:
    We praise you, O Lord.

10. All creatures,
    praise and glorify my Lord
    and give him thanks
    and serve him in great humility.
    WE PRAISE YOU, O LORD.

St. Francis of Assisi (1181–1226)
Trans. W.G.S.

Prayers for Light

A Spirit To Know You

Gracious and holy Father,
please give me:
intellect to understand you,
reason to discern you,
diligence to seek you,
wisdom to find you,
a spirit to know you,
a heart to meditate upon you,
ears to hear you,
eyes to see you,
a tongue to proclaim you,
a way of life pleasing to you,
patience to wait for you
and perseverance to look for you.
Grant me a perfect end—
your holy presence,
a blessed resurrection
and life everlasting.

Attributed to St. Benedict of Nursia (+555)

For Insight

May the Lord Jesus touch our eyes,
as he did those of the blind.
Then we shall begin to see
in visible things those which are invisible.
May he open our eyes to gaze,
not on present realities,
but on the blessings to come.
May he open the eyes of our heart
to contemplate God in Spirit,
through Jesus Christ the Lord, to whom
    belong
power and glory through all eternity.

Origen (185–253)

The Road Ahead

My Lord God,
I have no idea where I am going.
I do not see the road ahead of me.
I cannot know for certain where it will end.
Nor do I really know myself,
and the fact that I think that I am following
    your will does not mean
    that I am actually doing so.
But I believe that the desire to please you
    does in fact please you.
And I hope I have that desire in all that I am
    doing.
I hope that I will never do anything apart
    from that desire.

And I know that if I do this,
you will lead me by the right road though I
    may know nothing about it.
Therefore will I trust you always
though I may seem to be lost and in the
    shadow of death.
I will not fear, for you are ever with me,
and you will never leave me to face my perils
    alone.

Thomas Merton (1915–1968)

Flood the Path With Light

God of our life,
there are days when the burdens we carry
chafe our shoulders and weigh us down;
when the road seems dreary and endless,
the skies grey and threatening;
when our lives have no music in them,
and our hearts are lonely,
and our souls have lost their courage.
Flood the path with light,
turn our eyes to where the skies are full of
    promise;
tune our hearts to brave music;
give us the sense of comradeship
with heroes and saints of every age;
and so quicken our spirits
that we may be able to encourage
the souls of all who journey with us
on the road of life, to your honor and glory.

Attributed to St. Augustine (354–430)

For a Good Choice

Dear Father,
you are the creative origin of all I am
and of all I am called to be.
With the talents and opportunities I have,
how may I serve you best?
Please guide my mind and heart,
open me to the needs of my country and of
    the world,
and help me to choose wisely and practically
for your honor and glory
and for the good of all those whose lives I
    touch.

Make Your Light Shine

God our Father, you who said,
"Let there be light shining out of darkness,"
make your light shine in our hearts
so that the knowledge of the glory of God
which is on the face of Christ
may shine there also.

Throughout this day
may your mercy be our defense;
your praise, our gladness;
your Word, the treasure of our hearts.

Let your blessing descend on each of our
    actions.
Let it accompany us and help us reach
that great morning which knows no night,

when we will praise your love unceasingly,

through your Son Jesus Christ, our Savior
    and brother,
in the unity of the love of the Holy Spirit,
forever and ever.

Lucien Deiss

Truth and Beauty

God our Father,
by the work of your Spirit, living in our
    hearts,
you lead us to desire your perfection,
to seek for truth and to rejoice in beauty.

Enlighten and inspire
all thinkers, writers, artists and craftsmen,
so that in all things which are true and pure
    and beautiful,
your name may be made holy
and your kingdom come on earth.
We ask this through your Son Jesus Christ
    our Lord.

St. Anselm's Chapel, Canterbury Cathedral

Prayers for Families

For Families

O God our Father,
bind together in your all-embracing love
    every family on earth.
Banish anger and bitterness within them;
nourish forgiveness and peace.
Bestow upon parents such wisdom and
    patience
that they may gently exercise the disciplines
    of love,
and call forth from their children their
    greatest virtue and their highest skill.
Instill in children such independence and
    self-respect
that they may freely obey their parents,
and grow in the joys of companionship.
Open ears to hear the truth within the words
    another speaks;
open eyes to see the reality beneath another's
    appearance;
and make the mutual affection of families a
    sign of your kingdom;
through Jesus Christ our Lord.

From an Anglican Prayer Book

41

For Our Family

Father,
from whom all parenthood derives its
    meaning,
you created men and women
and blessed their union in marriage,
making them a help and support for each
    other.
Remember our family today,
help us to love one another unselfishly,
as Christ does his Church,
so that we may live together in joy and peace
and give you heartfelt praise,
through your Son and in the Holy Spirit.

For Our Household

O God of goodness and mercy,
 to your fatherly protection we commend
    our family,
    our household,
    and all that belongs to us.
We commit all to your love and keeping.
Fill this house with your blessings,
    even as you filled
    the house of Nazareth
    with your presence.

For Family Peace

Holy Father,
if any of us has any grievance against
    another,
may the sun not set on our anger
or disappointment,
but may we present as our offering to you
a forgiving heart.
Grant each of us the courage
to forgive those who have offended us,
the patience to bear with our own faults,
and the faith to renew our commitment to
    you
each day of the year.

Kevin Fleming

For Those We Love

Lord God,
we can hope for others nothing better
than the happiness we desire for ourselves.
Therefore, I pray you, do not separate me
    after death
from those I have tenderly loved on earth.
Grant that where I am they may be with me,
and that I may enjoy their presence in heaven
after being so often deprived of it on earth.
Lord God, I ask you to receive your beloved
    children
immediately into your life-giving heart.
After this brief life on earth,
give them eternal happiness.

St. Ambrose of Milan (334–397)

A Prayer For Husbands And Wives

Father, you called us to found this family
    together.
Give us the grace to animate it with your
    love;
May our family always comfort those who
    live in it and welcome those who enter it.
Through Christ our Lord.

The Pope's Family Prayer Book

For Our Children

Lord, help our children to know the road you
    have chosen for them:
may they give you glory and attain salvation.
Sustain them with your strength, and let
    them not be satisfied with easy goals.
Enlighten us, their parents,
that we may help them to recognize their
    calling in life and respond to it
    generously.
May we put no obstacle in the way of your
    inner guidance.

The Pope's Family Prayer Book

I Place Them in Your Care

Lord Jesus Christ,
I praise and thank you for my parents and
    my brothers and sisters
whom you have given me to cherish.
Surround them with your tender, loving
    care,
teach them to love and serve one another in
    true affection
and to look to you in all their needs.
I place them all in your care,
knowing that your love for them is greater
    than my own.
Keep us close to one another in this life
and conduct us at the last to our true and
    heavenly home.
Blessed be God forever.

For Parents in Trouble

Lord, you are present everywhere.
We ask your help for those of our parents
who are in trouble.
Where they are at odds with each other,
we pray for a breakthrough and
    reconciliation.
Where a job has been lost,
grant a new opportunity for useful work.
Where there is sickness,
we pray for healing and strength.
Where there are patterns which make life
    dull,
we pray for a broken routine
which will allow new possibilities.
O Lord,
some of our parents have trouble.
We ask you to help them,
and to help us to know what to do;
through Jesus Christ your Son.

John W. Vannorsdall

Take courage, toil and strive zealously, for
    nothing will be lost. Every prayer you
    make, every psalm you sing is recorded;
    every alms, every fast is recorded.
St. Cyril of Jerusalem

Prayers for the Human Family

For Love and Service

Lord,
you created us for yourself
and our hearts are restless until they rest in
    you.
Please show us how to love you with all our
    heart
and our neighbor as ourself.
Teach us to be practical about loving one
    another
in you and for you and as you desire.
Show us our immediate neighbor today;
call our attention to the needs of others.
Remind us that you count as done to you
what we do for one another,
and that our turning away from one another
is really turning our backs on you.
Make us know, love and serve you in this life
and be happy for ever in the next
in union with all our sisters and brothers,
children of a common Father.
To serve you is to reign.

For Service To Others

Make us worthy, Lord,
To serve our fellow human beings
      throughout the world who live and die
      in poverty and hunger.
Give them through our hands this day their
      daily bread,
And by our understanding love,
give peace and joy.

Mother Teresa of Calcutta

For Brotherhood

Father,
you have made us.
Red, yellow, brown, white and black,
tall and short, fat and thin,
rich and poor, young and old—
all are your children.
Teach us to cooperate rather than to compete,
to respect rather than to revile,
to forgive rather than to condemn.
Your Son turned from no one.
May we learn, like him, to be open
to the share of the divine
that you have implanted
in each of your sons and daughters.
And may we forge a bond of love
that will make a living reality
the brotherhood in which we profess to
      believe.

Christopher Prayers for Today

For the Needy

Grant, Lord, that I may gladly share
what I have with the needy,
humbly ask for what I need from him who
    has,
sincerely admit the evil I have done,
calmly bear the evil I suffer,
not envy my neighbor for his blessings,
and thank you unceasingly
whenever you hear my prayer.

St. Thomas Aquinas (1225–1274)

Let Us Not Be Blinded

O Lord,
do not let us turn into "broken cisterns"
that can hold no water . . .
do not let us be so blinded by the enjoyment
  of the good things of earth
that our hearts become insensible to the cry
    of the poor,
  of the sick, of orphaned children
    and of those innumerable brothers and
      sisters of ours
  who lack the necessary minimum to eat,
  to clothe their nakedness,
  and to gather their family together under
    one roof.

Pope John XXIII (1881–1963)

A Night Prayer For Those In Need

O God, before I sleep,
I remember before you all the people I love,
and now in the silence I say their names to
    you.
All the people who are sad and lonely, old
    and forgotten,
poor and hungry and cold,
in pain of body and in distress of mind.
Bless all who specially need your blessing,
and bless me, too,
and make this a good night for me.
This I ask for your love's sake.

William Barclay

Prayer is the key of morning and the bolt of
    evening.

Gandhi

For God's Good Earth

Father,
the bible tells us
you looked on all that you made
and saw that it was good.
But we have been too willing
to squander the richness of creation.
We have laid the ax to the mighty forests,
despoiled the green hillsides,
wasted earth's mineral wealth.
We have fouled the air,
littered the countryside
and polluted the streams and oceans.
Voices are raised
to stop us from squandering our patrimony.
May we heed them in time so that one day
we can look on the planet you have given us
and say with pride, once again,
"Behold, it is good."

Christopher Prayers for Today

For People of All Ages

Let us pray for our children:
  Help them to grow in grace and wisdom,
  and in the knowledge of your Son Jesus
    Christ.

Let us pray for our young men and women:
  Give them a full and happy youth;
  open their hearts to accept
  not only the suffering but also the joy of
    the world.

Let us pray for all married people
who have promised before Christ to be
faithful to each other:
May the fervor of their love show to the
world
the tenderness of Christ Jesus toward his
Church.

Let us pray for all those in the autumn of life:
Grant them a peaceful and happy old age;
guide their steps on the road to peace.

Let us pray for all those who have no family
and home:
Show the gentleness of your presence
to all who live alone
and have no hope but you.

Lucien Deiss

Prayers for Justice and Peace

Lord, Make Me an Instrument

Lord, make me an instrument of your peace:
    where there is hatred, let me sow love;
    where there is injury, pardon;
    where there is doubt, faith;
    where there is despair, hope;
    where there is darkness, light;
    and where there is sadness, joy.

O Divine Master, grant that I may not so
    much seek
to be consoled as to console,
to be understood as to understand,
to be loved as to love.

For it is in giving that we receive,
    it is in pardoning that we are pardoned,
    and it is in dying that we are born to
      eternal life.

Attributed to St. Francis of Assisi (1181–1226)

Prayer for Peace

O God, from whom proceed
  all holy desires,
  all right counsels
  and all just works,
give unto your servants that peace which the
    world cannot give,
that our hearts may be set to obey your
    commandments,
  and, being delivered from the fear of our
    enemies,
we may pass our time
  under your protection
  in peace and rest.
Through Christ our Lord.

For Reconciliation

Lord God,
out of your great love for the world,
you reconciled earth to heaven
through your only-begotten Son our Savior.
In the darkness of our sins,
we fail to love one another as we should;
please pour your light into our souls
and fill us with your tenderness
that we may embrace our friends in you
and our enemies for your sake,
in a bond of mutual affection.
We make our prayer through the same Christ
    our Lord.

Visigothic Liturgy

Prayer for Concord

God the Father,
origin of all that is divine,
good beyond all that is good,
fair beyond all that is fair,
in you is calmness, peace and concord.
Heal what divides us from one another
and bring us back into the unity of love,
bearing some likeness to your divine nature.
Through the embrace of love
and the bonds of godly affection,
make us one in the Spirit
by that peace of yours that makes all things
    peaceful.
We ask this through the grace, mercy and
    tenderness
of your only begotten Son, Jesus Christ our
    Lord.

St. Dionysius of Alexandria (+264)

For Our Nation

Eternal God,
have mercy on the faithful
for whom our Lord and Savior Jesus Christ
poured out his precious blood.
Through your only-begotten Son
avert the dangers which threaten
our people and country.

St. Peter Canisius (1521–1597)

For Civil Authorities

Almighty and ever-living God,
  in whose hand are the rights and hopes of
    every people,
Look graciously on those who govern,
  that in lasting peace they may promote
    social progress and religious freedom
  for all the nations of the earth.
Through Christ our Lord.

The Pope's Family Prayer Book

A Prayer for Peacemakers

O Lord, God of peace,
you have created us and shown us your love
so that we may share in your glory.
We bless you and give thanks
because you have sent us Jesus, your
    well-beloved Son.
Through the mystery of his resurrection,
you made him the worker of salvation,
the source of peace, the bond of brotherhood.

We give thanks for the desires, efforts and
    achievements
stirred up by the Spirit of peace in our time,
to replace hate by love, mistrust by
    understanding,
indifference by interdependence.

Open our minds and hearts to the real
    demands of love,
so that we may become more completely
    peacemakers.

Remember, Father of mercy,
all who struggle, suffer and die
to bring forth a world of closer relationship.
May your kingdom of justice, peace and love
come to people of every race and tongue.
May the earth be filled with your glory.

Pope Paul VI (1897–1978)

Peace in Our Days

Almighty and eternal God,
may your grace enkindle in all
a love for the many unfortunate people
    whom poverty and misery reduce to a
        condition of life
    unworthy of human beings.
Arouse in the hearts of those who call you
        Father
a hunger and thirst for justice and peace,
    and for fraternal charity in deeds and in
        truth.
Grant, O Lord, peace in our days,
peace to souls, peace to families, peace to our
        country,
and peace among nations.

Pope Pius XII (1876–1958)

Prayers for the Church

For the Church

Gracious Father,
we pray to you for your holy Catholic
    Church.
Fill it with your truth.
Keep it in your peace.
Where it is corrupt, reform it.
Where it is in error, correct it.
Where it is right, defend it.
Where it is in want, provide for it.
Where it is divided, reunite it;
for the sake of your Son, our Savior Jesus
    Christ.

William Laud (+1645)

For the Church of Your Son Jesus

God our Father, we pray to you
for the Church of your Son Jesus.

Let her be resplendent
with the beauty of Jesus;
let her avoid painting herself
with the vain beauty of the world.

Let her not be disfigured
by the wrinkles of old age;
let her represent for all people
the hope of the future.

Let her face be purified
from every stain of pride;
let her show preference
for the poor and the humble.

Let her be holy and spotless;
let her not be maimed by error.

Let her be beautiful as one betrothed,
all dressed up for her spouse;
let her shun the unseemly "adornments"
of money and power.

Lord Jesus,
you have loved your Church,
and you have given yourself up for her;
we pray to you:

Guide this Church that she, in turn,
will love all people,
and put herself at their service.

Lucien Deiss

For the Pope

Almighty Father in heaven,
shelter under your protective care
our holy father, the Pope.
Direct him according to your loving kindness
in the way of eternal salvation
for all of us.

Lord Jesus, the one true shepherd,
guide the Pope
in the care of your people on earth.

Through the Holy Spirit
which you have given him
be his light, his strength
and his consolation.

Through your help
may he ever teach the truth
and accomplish always
what is pleasing to you,
O Holy Trinity!

For Our Bishop

O God, you sent the Lord Jesus for the good
of the whole world.
Through him you chose the apostles,
and after them, from one generation to
another,
you have ordained for us saintly bishops.

God of truth, fill our bishop, N., with life,
and make him a worthy successor of the
      apostles.
Give him grace and the power of the Holy
      Spirit,
the Spirit you gave so generously to your
      servants, the prophets and patriarchs.
Make him a worthy shepherd of your flock,
living as our bishop, blamelessly and without
      offense.

Serapion's Prayer Book (4th century)

The Good Shepherd

Gather together your sheep, Lord,
in all the places where they have been
      scattered
during the mist and darkness.

Lead them to good pasturage,
let them rest in good grazing ground.

Those who are lost—search out;
those who have strayed—bring back.

Those who are wounded—bind their
      wounds;
those who are sick—cure.

Those bearing young—watch over them;
all of your sheep—keep them safe in your
      flock.

Lord Jesus,
because you are our good shepherd,
help us all to be the sheep of your flock.

Gather all into the fold of your love
so that there may be but one flock
   and only one shepherd.

Lucien Deiss

Prayer for Vocations

God our Father,
you will all to be saved
and come to the knowledge of the truth.
Send workers into your harvest
that the gospel may be preached to every
   creature
and your people, gathered together by the
   word of life
and strengthened by the power of the
   sacraments,
may advance in the way of salvation and
   love.
Please grant this through Christ our Lord.

The Christian ideal has not been tried and
   found wanting. It has been found
   difficult and left untried.

G. K. Chesterton

Prayers for Strength

Like Children

Like children playing on the beach
we have built houses of sand.
The wave of time has come
and the laughter of the tides has submerged
    everything.

But we know, Lord,
that if our earthly home is destroyed
you will build us an eternal home near you in
    heaven.

Give us strength to leave our earthly
    dwellings
  and our games in the sand.
Direct our boat
toward the shores of eternity.

Lucien Deiss

For Courage

Lord Jesus, teach me to be generous;
teach me to serve you as you deserve,
to give and not to count the cost,
to fight and not to heed the wounds,
to toil and not to seek for rest,
to labor and not to seek reward,
except that of knowing that I do your will.

St. Ignatius Loyola (1491–1556)

Into Your Hands

Father,
I abandon myself into your hands;
do with me what you will.
Whatever you may do, I thank you:
I am ready for all, I accept all.
Let only your will be done in me,
and in all your creatures—
I wish no more than this, O Lord.
Into your hands I commend my soul;
I offer it to you with all the love of my heart,
for I love you, Lord, and so need to give
     myself,
to surrender myself into your hands without
     reserve,
and with boundless confidence,
for you are my Father.

Charles de Foucauld (1858–1916)

Light Up the Small Duties

O Father, light up
the small duties of this day's life:
may they shine
with the beauty of your countenance.
May we believe that glory can dwell
in the commonest task of every day.

St. Augustine (354–430)

For Perseverance

O Lord,
keep us from the vain strife of words
and help us profess the truth.
Preserve us in the faith,
true faith and undefiled,
that we may always hold fast
what we promised when we were baptized
in the Name of the Father, the Son and the
     Holy Spirit.
May we have you for our Father,
and may we always live in your Son
and in the fellowship of the Holy Spirit,
through the same Christ Jesus our Lord.

St. Hilary of Poitiers (+368)

Now Let Me Accept

O heavenly Father,
I praise and thank you for the peace of the
     night;

I praise and thank you for this new day;
I praise and thank you for all your goodness
and faithfulness throughout my life.

You have granted me many blessings.
Now let me also accept what is hard
from your hand.
You will lay on me no more that I can bear.
You make all things work together
for the good of your children.

Dietrich Bonhoeffer (1906–1945)

A Prayer to the Holy Cross

By you hell is despoiled, O Holy Cross.
By you its mouth is stopped up to all the
redeemed.
By you demons are made afraid and
restrained,
conquered and trampled under foot.
By you the world is renewed
and made beautiful with truth,
governed by the light of righteousness.
By you sinful humanity is justified,
the condemned are saved,
the servants of sin and hell are set free,
the dead are raised to life.
By you the blessed city in heaven
is restored and made perfect.
By you God, the Son of God willed for our
sakes

"to become obedient to the Father, even
    unto death,"
Because of which he is exalted and has
    received
"the Name which is above every other
    name."
By you "his throne is prepared"
    and his kingdom established.

St. Anselm of Canterbury (1033–1109)

Prayer to Michael the Archangel

Holy Michael the Archangel, defend us in
    battle.
Be our protection against the wickedness and
    snares of the devil.
May God rebuke him, we humbly pray,
and do thou, O Prince of the heavenly host,
by the power of God,
thrust into hell Satan and all wicked spirits
who wander through the world for the ruin
    of souls.

Do what you can and then pray that God will
    give you the power to do what you
    cannot.

St. Augustine

Prayers in Time of Illness

Raise Me Up, Lord

Raise me up, Lord, do not abandon your
  servant.
I want health that I may sing to you
  and help your people lead holy lives.
I plead with you: you are my strength,
  do not desert me.
I have grown weak amid the storm
  but I long to return to you.

St. Gregory of Nazianzus (329–389)

Lord Jesus, Healer

Lord Jesus, healer of our souls and bodies,
during your life on earth,
you went about doing good,
healing every manner of sickness and
  disease,
strengthening, curing, comforting and
  consoling.
You want nothing more than to see us
  healthy and happy.
You are the enemy of death and disease,
and in and through you they are overcome
  and conquered.
Lay your healing hands upon us now,
so that we may live in your praise untiringly.

For Recovery From Sickness

God of heavenly power,
one word from you can free us from every
    weakness and disease.
Kindly hear our prayers,
free us from our sickness,
restore our health,
and give us the vigor to praise you
    unceasingly.
We ask this through Christ our Lord.

Gallican Liturgy (7th century)

For the Sick

Father, your only Son took upon himself
  the sufferings and weakness of the whole
    human race;
through his passion and cross
  he taught us how good can be brought out
  of suffering.
Look upon our brothers and sisters who are
    ill.
In the midst of illness and pain,
may they be united with Christ, who heals
    both body and soul;
may they know the consolation promised to
    those who suffer
  and be fully restored to health.
Through Christ our Lord.

The Pope's Family Prayer Book

In Time of Sickness

Lord Jesus,
you suffered and died for me;
you understand suffering and you share it
    with us.
Teach me to accept my pains,
to bear them in union with you,
and to offer them up for the forgiveness of
    my sins
and for the welfare of the living and the
    dead.
Calm my fears, increase my trust in you;
make me patient and cooperative with those
    who serve me,
and if it be your will,
please restore me to health,
so that I may work for your honor and glory
and for the salvation of all.

In Time of Serious Illness

God, Our Father, Eternal Mystery,
I believe in your boundless,
    unchanging love.

You have created me for yourself,
    to enjoy your peace and love
    for all eternity.

Help me to overcome my failings,
    my fear of suffering,
    my dread of the unknown.

I will do all in my power to improve
or regain my health, and fulfill
all the obligations of my state
in life, particularly to
those nearest me.

Bring me finally to perfect union
with your will.

I accept now the time, place, and
manner of my death, knowing it is
but a change to an infinitely
better life with you.

Yes, Lord, I want to serve you.
Yes, I want to be with you.

Robert L. Mutchler

Your Will Be Done

God and loving Father,
your will be done.
I offer my sickness with all its suffering to
you,
together with all that my Savior has suffered
for me.
By the power of his blessed passion,
have mercy on me
and free me from this illness and pain
if it be according to your will
and for my good.
Lord, I entrust my life and my death to you;

do with me as you please.
In sickness and in health,
I only want to love you always.

Prayer to Mary for the Sick

Mary, health of the sick,

Be at the bedside of all the world's sick
    people;
  of those who are unconscious and dying;
  of those who have begun their agony;
  of those who have abandoned all hope of a
    cure;
  of those who weep and cry out in pain:
  of those who cannot receive care
  because they have no money;
  of those who ought to be resting
  but are forced by poverty to work;
  of those who seek vainly in their beds
  for a less painful position;
  of those who pass long nights sleepless;
  of those who are tormented
  by the cares of a family in distress;
  of those who must renounce
  their most cherished plans for the future;
  of those, above all,
  who do not believe in a better life;
  of those who rebel and curse God;
  of those who do not know that Christ
  suffered like them and for them.

Rabboni

Prayers for the Journey

You Are Waiting To Surprise Us

God our Father,
you are waiting in the future to surprise us
    with love.
Help us to welcome you with joy whenever
    you appear,
so that we may live like excited children,
    always expecting you.
Through Jesus Christ our Lord.

Let My Soul Take Refuge

O thou full of compassion,
I commit and commend myself unto thee,
in whom I am, and live, and know.
Be thou the goal of my pilgrimage,
and my rest by the way.
Let my soul take refuge from the crowding
    turmoil
of worldly thought beneath the shadow of
    thy wings;
Let my heart, this sea of restless waves,
find peace in thee, O God.

St. Augustine (354–430)

Now That I Have Found You

Like a thirsty child reaching for a drink,
I grasp for you, O God.
And I have found you.
I have sensed your holy presence in the
    worship service;
And in the hour of prayer I have felt you to
    be near.
I realize now that your love for me is far
    better than life itself.

My heart is full of joy and contentment.
My mouth is filled with praises for you.
Even the night hours are no longer lonely
As I contemplate your tender concern for me.

The enemies of my soul still seek to betray
    me,
But they shall not snatch me out of your
    hand.
And now that I have found you,
I shall be secure and happy forever.

Leslie F. Brandt (Paraphrase on Psalm 63)

God of Our Childhood

God of our childhood,
you whose name we have learned
in the smiles of our father and mother,
    we beg you:
Preserve in us a childlike spirit
so that we can enter your Kingdom.

74

God of our adolescence,
you who have created the eagerness of
    youth,
who know its desires and its follies,
  we beg you:
Preserve the flower of hope in our hearts,
be always the God of the joy of our youth.

God of our maturity,
you who call each man
to make fruitful the gifts you have put in
    him,
  we beg you:
Help each of us to become that perfect Man
who realizes the fullness of Christ.

God of our old age,
at the time when the spirit loses its ardor,
when the body becomes feeble,
  we beg you:
Remain close to us when the night comes.
You are our God for all eternity.

Lucien Deiss

In the twilight of life, God will not judge us
    on our earthly possessions and human
    success, but rather on how much we
    have loved.

St. John of the Cross

"Fear Not, for I Have Redeemed You"

Thus says the Lord:

He who created you, O Jacob
He who formed you, O Israel:

"Fear not, for I have redeemed you;
I have called you by name and you are mine.
When you pass through the waters
    I will be with you
and through the rivers,
    they shall not overwhelm you;
when you walk through fire
    you shall not be burned, and
    the flame shall not consume you.
For I am the Lord your God
the Holy One of Israel, your Savior.
And you are precious in my eyes,
    and cherished,
    and I love you."

Isaiah 43: 1–4 (RSV)

I Have Spent My Life, Lord

I have spent my life, Lord,
tuning up my lyre
instead of singing to you.
   I'm sorry, Lord.

I have spent my life, Lord,
looking for my own path
instead of walking with you.
   I'm sorry, Lord.

I have spent my life, Lord,
begging for love
instead of loving you in my brothers.
   I'm sorry, Lord.

I have spent my life, Lord,
fleeing the night
instead of saying: You are my light.
   I'm sorry, Lord.

I have spent my life, Lord,
seeking security
instead of placing my hand in yours.
   I'm sorry, Lord.

I have spent my life, Lord,
making resolutions
and not keeping them.
   I'm sorry, Lord.

Now, if it is true, Lord,
that you save us
not because of our works
but because of your great mercy,
then we are now ready
to receive your salvation.

Lucien Deiss

Prayers Near Journey's End

For the Aged

Eternal Father, unchanged down the
     changing years,
be near to those who are aged.
Even though their bodies weaken,
   grant that their spirit may be strong.
May they bear weariness and affliction with
     patience,
   and at the end, meet death with serenity.
Through Christ our Lord.

The Pope's Family Prayer Book

For the Dying

Lord,
this night some will be gathered to the
     Father.
Grant that they may go forth
surrounded by their loved ones,
without pain of body,
with clarity of mind,
and joyful expectancy of soul.

J. M. Ford

Stay With Us, Lord

Stay with us, Lord:
Behold, evening is coming,
and we still haven't recognized your face
in each of our brothers and sisters.
Stay with us, Lord Jesus Christ!

Stay with us, Lord:
behold, evening is coming,
and we still haven't shared your bread
in thanksgiving with all our brothers and
    sisters.
Stay with us, Lord Jesus Christ!

Stay with us, Lord:
behold, evening is coming,
and we still haven't recognized your Word
in the words of all our brothers and sisters.
Stay with us, Lord Jesus Christ!

Stay with us, Lord:
behold, evening is coming,
and our hearts are still too slow to believe
that you had to die in order to rise again.
Stay with us, Lord Jesus Christ!

Stay with us, Lord,
for our night itself becomes day
    when you are there!
Stay with us, Lord Jesus Christ!

Lucien Deiss

Prayer for a Happy Death

Lord Jesus Christ,
you want everyone's salvation
and no one ever appeals to you in vain,
for with your own lips you promised:
"Whatever you ask the Father in my name, I
    will do."
In your name—Jesus, Savior—
I ask that in my dying moments
you will give me full use of my senses,
heart-felt sorrow for my sins,
firm faith, hope in good measure and perfect
    love,
that I may be able to say
    honestly to you:
"Into your hands, O Lord, I commend my
    spirit.
You have redeemed me, Lord God of truth."

St. Vincent Ferrer (1350–1419)

Come to Me Like a Cry of Joy

When my life sinks in sadness,
come to me like a cry of joy.
    Come, Lord Jesus Christ!

When my heart is as hard as a rock,
come to me like the dew of springtime.
    Come, Lord Jesus Christ!

When noise invades my haven,
come to me like an oasis of silence.
Come, Lord Jesus Christ!

When the wind of hate rises within me,
come to me like a kiss of pardon.
Come, Lord Jesus Christ!

When I am sinking into the darkness of
death,
come to me like a child's smile.
Come, Lord Jesus Christ!

And when the earth encloses me in its arms,
open for me the doors of your mercy.
Come, Lord Jesus Christ!

Lucien Deiss

For the Gift of Final Perseverance

I pray you, noble Jesus,
that as you have graciously granted me
joyfully to imbibe the words of your
knowledge,
so you will also of your bounty
grant me to come at length to you,
the fount of all wisdom,
and to dwell in your presence
for ever.

St. Bede the Venerable (673–735)

For the Faithful Departed

By the merits of your rising from the dead,
    Lord Christ,
let death no longer have dominion
over the faithful departed.
Grant to your servants
a resting place in your eternal mansions
and in the arms of Abraham,
    our father in the faith.
Grant this to all who,
from Adam and Eve to this day,
have served you with a clean heart—
to our mothers and fathers,
to our sisters and brothers,
to our friends and kindred.
Make a place in your heavenly kingdom,
    Lord,
for everyone who has done you faithful
    service
in this present life
and to all who, in their fashion,
have striven toward you.

An Ancient Prayer

For Those Who Have Gone Before Us

The Lord will open to them the gates of
    paradise,
and they will return to that homeland
where there is no death, but only
    lasting joy.

Give them eternal rest, O Lord,
    and let them share your glory.

O God, our Creator and Redeemer,
by your power Christ conquered death
and returned to you in glory.
May all your people who have gone
    before us in faith
share his victory
and enjoy the vision of your glory for
    ever,
where Christ lives and reigns with you
    and the Holy Spirit,
one God, for ever and ever.

Roman Missal

And Peace At Last

May he support us all the day long,
till the shadows lengthen
and the evening comes
and the busy world is hushed
and the fever of life is over
and our work is done—
then in his mercy—
may he give us a safe lodging
and a holy rest
and peace at the last.

Attributed to John Henry Newman (1801–1890)

Holy Scripture is the table of Christ, from whence we are nourished, from whence we learn what we should love and what we should desire, to whom we should have our eyes raised.

Alcuin of York

3. The Week With Christ

SUNDAY—Blessed Trinity

MONDAY—Holy Spirit

TUESDAY—All Saints
　　　　　Faithful Departed

WEDNESDAY—St. Joseph

THURSDAY—Blessed Sacrament

FRIDAY—Holy Cross
　　　　Sacred Heart

SATURDAY—Blessed Virgin Mary

You do not enter into Paradise tomorrow or the day after or in years: You enter it today when you are poor and crucified.

Leon Bloy

Days of the Lord

FROM THE VERY BEGINNING of their existence as a people, Christians have dedicated days of the week to the several mysteries of their redemption so that by meditating on them one by one they might enter more and more deeply into their meaning and their saving power. In recent centuries the dedications used here have become widespread among Catholics.

On the *Lord's Day*, we commemorate the Blessed Trinity: God as a family of co-equal persons, the sum total of all the mysteries of faith. The many incidents and layers of meaning to be found in the Lord's Day—Easter, Pentecost, Parousia—are fulfilled in the worship of the Triune God who is ever active on our behalf. YHWH is the Name of our God: God-for-us, God-with-us, God-on-our-side.

On *Monday*, we concentrate upon the work of the Holy Spirit, the active presence of God in our hearts and in our Christian families and communities. He pours forth the love of God in our hearts, inspires us to perpetual prayer, and guides us into all truth, as Jesus promised. Come, Holy Spirit!

On *Tuesday*, we commemorate all who have fallen asleep in Christ, both those who have achieved the fullness of faith and devotion (the saints) and those who still need our prayers in the communion of saints (the souls in purgatory). The fellowship of faith knows no boundaries of time and space.

On *Wednesday*, we pause to honor St. Joseph, the husband of Mary, the foster father of Jesus, the humble, hard-working carpenter of Nazareth. We see in him complete trust in God, unquestioning obedience, and total dedication to the welfare of others. He is the special patron of those who labor with their hands and of the universal Church.

On *Thursday*, our thoughts turn to the Blessed Sacrament of the Altar, instituted at the Last Supper on Holy Thursday evening. It is the fulfillment of the many sacrifices of the Old Law, the present celebration of the people of the New Covenant, and the anticipation of the final in-gathering when all God's children will sit down at the welcome table of the eternal and heavenly banquet.

On *Friday*, we commemorate the suffering of Jesus who freely accepted death for us all and now reigns in glory as the Lord of life.

Love is the only explanation for his total self-giving on our behalf. His pierced heart is the guarantee of our salvation: it is the undying source of the saving waters of baptism and of the chalice of salvation from which we all drink. Nothing can separate us from the love of God revealed in Christ!

On *Saturday*, we recall Mary's role in our salvation. God-is-with-us (Emmanuel) through the free consent and cooperation of the Blessed Virgin Mary. She treasured all the incidents of the incarnation and "meditated on them in her heart" (Lk 2:19); she stood upright at the foot of the cross, the mother of sorrows, our lady of compassion (Jn 19:25); at Pentecost she was present in the upper room at the birth of the Church (Acts 1:14). She is the mother of Christ, the mother of the Church, the mother of each believing soul.

Praying in this way—morning, noon and evening—"we shall be spared the possibility of temptation and spiritual ruin, since we remember Christ at all times" (Hippolytus of Rome, *The Apostolic Tradition*, 41).

In group recitation, the stanzas of the psalms and canticles may be alternated between the leader and the group *or* the group may divide in two and alternate the stanzas between the two halves. All recite the antiphons before and after the psalms and canticles.

Sunday—The Blessed Trinity

MORNING

O Lord, + open my lips.
—And my mouth will proclaim your praise.

Psalm 8 God's Glory and Our Human
                    Dignity

Antiphon Blessed be the Creator and
                    Governor of all things,
                    the Holy and Undivided Trinity,
                    now and always and for ever and
                    ever.

Lord, our Lord,
    your greatness is seen in all the world!
Your praise reaches up to the heavens;
    it is sung by children and babies.
You have built a fortress against your foes
    to stop your enemies and adversaries.

When I look at the sky, which you have
     made,
   at the moon and the stars, which you set in
      their places—
what are human beings that you think of
      them;
   mere humans, that you care for them?

Yet you made them inferior only to yourself;
   you crowned them with glory and honor.
You made them ruler over all you have made;
   you placed them over all things:
sheep and cattle,
   and wild animals too;
the birds and the fish,
   and all the creatures in the seas.

Lord, our Lord,
   your greatness is seen in all the world!

Glory to the Father, and to the Son, and to
   the Holy Spirit:
   as it was in the beginning, is now, and will
   be for ever. Amen.

Ant. Blessed be the Creator and Governor of
            all things,
            the Holy and Undivided Trinity,
            now and always and for ever and
            ever.

Psalm Prayer

Blessed Trinity,
as we contemplate your majesty displayed in
    the heavens,
help us to honor our dignity as human
    creatures
and to co-operate with you for the good of
    all.
Please grant this through Christ Jesus our
    Lord.
—Amen.

Reading   *Romans 11:33–36*

How great are God's riches! How deep are his
wisdom and knowledge! Who can explain his
decisions? Who can understand his ways? As
the scripture says, "Who knows the mind of
the Lord? Who is able to give him advice?
Who has ever given him anything, so that he
had to pay it back?" For all things were
created by him, and all things exist through
him and for him. To God be the glory for ever!
Amen.

Response

Let us bless the Father, the Son and the Holy
    Spirit.
—Let us praise and glorify God for ever.

Canticle of Zachary

Luke 1:68–79

Ant. Holy, holy, holy is the Lord God
        Almighty,
    who was, who is, and who is to come,
    alleluia.

Blessed + be the Lord, the God of Israel;
  he has come to his people and set them
    free.
He has raised up for us a mighty Savior,
  born of the house of his servant David.

Through his holy prophets he promised of
    old
  that he would save us from our enemies,
  from the hands of all who hate us.
He promised to show mercy to our ancestors
  and to remember his holy covenant.

This was the oath he swore to our father
    Abraham:
  to set us free from the hands of our
    enemies,
free to worship him without fear,
  holy and righteous in his sight
  all the days of our life.

You, my child, shall be called the prophet of
 the Most High;
 for you will go before the Lord to prepare
 his way,
to give his people knowledge of salvation
 by the forgiveness of their sins.

In the tender compassion of our God
 the dawn from on high shall break upon
 us,
to shine on those who dwell in darkness and
 the shadow of death,
 and to guide our feet into the way of peace.

Glory to the Father, in the Son, through the
 Spirit:
 now and for ever.   Amen.

Ant. Holy, holy, holy is the Lord God
 Almighty,
 who was, who is, and who is to come,
 alleluia.

Collect Prayer

Father,
You sent your Word to bring us truth
and your Spirit to make us holy.
Through them we come to know the mystery
 of your life.

Help us to worship you, one God in three
      Persons,
by proclaiming and living our faith in you.
Grant this through our Lord Jesus Christ,
      your Son,
who lives and reigns with you and the Holy
      Spirit,
one God, for ever and ever.
—Amen.

Blessing

May almighty God, the Father, + the Son
      and the Holy Spirit, bless and keep us.
—Amen.

NOON

Come, let us worship the true God:
—One in Three and Three in One.

Reading

Our great Father, God almighty, who is
Being, knew and loved us from eternity.
Through his knowledge, and in the
marvelous depths of his charity, together
with the foresight and wisdom of the whole
blessed Trinity, he willed that the Second
Person should become our Mother, Brother,
and Savior. Hence it follows that God is as

96

truly our Mother as he is our Father. Our
Father decides, our Mother works, our good
Lord, the Holy Spirit, strengthens. So we
ought to love our God in whom we have our
own being, reverently thanking him, and
praising him for creating us, earnestly
beseeching our Mother for mercy and pity,
and our Lord, the Spirit, for help and grace.
For in these three is contained our life:
nature, mercy, grace. From these we get our
humility, gentleness, patience and pity.

Julian of Norwich (1342–1416)
Revelations of Divine Love

Response

You are God: we praise you;
You are the Lord: we acclaim you;
You are the eternal Father:
All creation worships you.

To you all angels, all the powers of heaven,
Cherubim and Seraphim, sing in endless
    praise:
  Holy, holy, holy Lord, God of power and
    might,
  heaven and earth are full of your glory.

The glorious company of apostles praise you.
The noble fellowship of prophets praise you.
The white-robed army of martyrs praise you.

Throughout the world the holy Church
    acclaims you:
  Father, of majesty unbounded,
  your true and only Son, worthy of all
    worship,
  and the Holy Spirit, advocate and guide.

Te Deum Laudamus

Prayer

To God the Father,
who loves us and made us accepted in the
    Beloved:
To God the Son,
who loved us and loosed us from our sins by
    his own blood:
To God the Holy Spirit,
who sheds the love of God abroad in our
    hearts:
To the one true God,
be all love and glory for time and for eternity.
Amen.

EVENING

O God, + come to my assistance.
—O Lord, make haste to help me.

Psalm 100 A Hymn of Praise to the Holy
            Trinity

Ant. Come, let us adore the true God, One in
        Three and Three in One.

Sing for joy to the Lord, all the world!
    Worship the Lord gladly,
    and come before him with joyful songs!

Never forget that the Lord is God!
    He made us, and we belong to him;
    we are his people, we are his flock.

Enter his temple with thanksgiving,
    go into his sanctuary with praise!
    Give thanks to him and praise him!

The Lord is good;
    his love lasts for ever,
    and his faithfulness for all time.

Glory to the Father, and to the Son, and to
    the Holy Spirit:
    as it was in the beginning, is now, and will
    be for ever.   Amen.

THE WEEK WITH CHRIST

Ant. Come, let us adore the true God, One in Three and Three in One.

Psalm Prayer

Almighty and everlasting God,
to whom we owe the grace of professing the true faith,
grant that while acknowledging the glory of the eternal Trinity
and adoring its majestic unity,
we may be confirmed in this faith
and defended against all adversities.
We ask this through Jesus Christ our Lord,
who lives and reigns with you and the Holy Spirit,
one God, for ever and ever.
—Amen.

Reading   *Titus 3:6–7*

God poured out the Holy Spirit abundantly on us, through Jesus Christ our Savior, so that by his grace we might be put right with God and come into possession of the eternal life we hope for.

Response

Holy, holy, holy Lord, God of power and might.
—Heaven and earth are full of your glory.

Canticle of Mary   *Luke 1: 46–55*

Ant. All things were created by God,
        all things exist through God,
        all things are for God, alleluia.

My soul + proclaims the greatness of the
        Lord;
    my spirit rejoices in God my Savior
    for he has looked with favor on his lowly
        servant.

From this day all generations will call me
        blessed:
    the Almighty has done great things for me,
    and holy is his Name.
He has mercy on those who fear him
    in every generation.

He has shown the strength of his arm,
    he has scattered the proud in their conceit.
He has cast down the mighty from their
        thrones,
    and has lifted up the lowly.
He has filled the hungry with good things,
    and the rich he has sent away empty.

He has come to the help of his servant Israel
  for he has remembered his promise of
      mercy,
the promise he made to our ancestors,
  to Abraham and Sarah and their children
      for ever.

Glory to the Father, in the Son, through the
      Spirit:
  now and for ever.   Amen.

Ant. All things were created by God,
        all things exist through God,
        all things are for God, alleluia.

Collect Prayer

God, we praise you:
Father all-powerful, Christ Lord and Savior,
  Spirit of love.
You reveal yourself in the depths of our
      being,
drawing us to share in your life and your
      love.
One God, three Persons,
be near to the people formed in your image,
close to the world your love brings to life.
We ask this, Father, Son, and Holy Spirit,
One God, true and living, for ever and ever.
—Amen.

Blessing

May the grace of our Lord Jesus Christ + and
   the love of God and the fellowship of the
   Holy Spirit be with us all.
—Amen.

Monday—The Holy Spirit

MORNING

O Lord, + open my lips.
—And my mouth will proclaim your praise.

Psalm 104 In Praise of God the Creator
and Renewer

Ant. Send forth your Spirit, O Lord, and
renew the face of the earth.

O Lord, my God, how supreme is your
greatness;
you are clothed with majesty and glory.
You robe yourself with a mantle of light,
and stretch out the heavens like a curtain.

How manifold are your works, O Lord!
In wisdom you have made them all;
the earth is full of your creatures.
And there is the sea, vast and wide,
with its swarms of living things without
number,
creatures both great and small.

All of them look to you
  to give them their food in due season.
When you give it to them, they gather it;
  when you open your hand, they are filled
    with good.

When you hide your face, they are troubled;
  when you take away their breath,
  they die and return to dust.
When you send forth your Spirit, they are
    created,
  and you renew the face of the earth.

The glory of the Lord is everlasting;
  the Lord rejoices in his works.
I will sing to the Lord as long as I live;
  I will praise my God as long as I breathe.

Glory to the Father, and to the Son, and to
    the Holy Spirit:
  as it was in the beginning, is now, and will
    be for ever.   Amen.

Ant. Send forth your Spirit, O Lord, and
    renew the face of the earth.

Psalm Prayer

Father of light,
you continually renew our lives
by fresh infusions of the Holy Spirit.

We praise you for all your gifts
and ask for the full revelation of your will.
Please grant this through Jesus our Lord.
—Amen.

Reading

Acts 5:30–32

The God of our ancestors raised Jesus from
death, after you had killed him by nailing him
to a cross. God raised him to his right side as
Leader and Savior, to give to the people of
Israel the opportunity to repent and have their
sins forgiven. We are witnesses to these
things—we and the Holy Spirit, who is God's
gift to those who obey him.

Response

The Apostles were all filled with the Holy
  Spirit.
—And began to speak as the Spirit prompted
  them.

Canticle of Zachary See page 94.

Ant. Receive the Holy Spirit. When you
  forgive sins they are forgiven,
  alleluia.

Collect Prayer

God our Father,
let the Spirit you sent on your Church
to begin the teaching of the Gospel
continue to work in the world
through the hearts of all who believe.
We make our prayer through Christ our
Lord.
—Amen.

Blessing

May the Holy Spirit, the Lord and Giver of
life, + bless and keep us.
—Amen.

NOON

The Spirit of the Lord fills the whole world.
—Come, let us adore him.

Reading

"The Spirit of wisdom and understanding, the
Spirit of counsel and strength, the Spirit of
knowledge and the fear of God" (Isaiah 11:2)
came down upon the Lord, and the Lord in
turn gave this Spirit to his Church, sending
the Advocate from heaven into all the world

into which, according to his words, the devil too had been cast down like lightning. If we are not to be scorched and made unfruitful, we need the dew of God. Since we have our accuser, we need an Advocate as well. And so the Lord in his pity for us, who had fallen into the hands of brigands, having himself bound up our wounds and left for our care two coins bearing the imperial image, entrusted us to the Holy Spirit. Now, through the Spirit, the image and inscription of the Father and the Son have been given to us, and it is our duty to use the coin committed to our charge and make it yield a rich profit for the Lord.

St. Irenaeus (+203), Against Heresies, *III*, 17.

Response

O Holy Spirit, by whose breath
 Life rises vibrant out of death:
 Come to create, renew, inspire;
 Come, kindle in our hearts your fire.

You are the seeker's sure resource,
 Of burning love the living source,
 Protector in the midst of strife,
 The giver and the Lord of life.

In you God's energy is shown,
  To us your varied gifts made known.
  Teach us to speak, teach us to hear;
  Yours is the tongue and yours the ear.

Flood our dull senses with your light;
  In mutual love our hearts unite.
  Your power the whole creation fills;
  Confirm our weak, uncertain wills.

From inner strife grant us release;
  Turn nations to the ways of peace,
  To fuller life your people bring
  That as one body we may sing:

Praise to the Father, Christ his Word,
  And to the Spirit, God the Lord;
  To them all honor, glory be
  Both now and for eternity.
Amen.

Veni, Creator Spiritus
Trans. John Webster Grant

Prayer

Holy Spirit of truth,
Sovereign Lord of the universe,
guide and guardian of your people,
present everywhere,
overflowing all that exists:
Come and dwell in us,

cleanse us from all sin,
pour out your blessings on us,
give us fresh life,
and in your gracious love
bring us to salvation.

Byzantine Liturgy

EVENING

O God, + come to my assistance.
—O Lord, make haste to help me.

Psalm 29   The Spirit Over the Waters

Ant. From heaven came a sound of rushing
wind, and there appeared to them
fiery tongues.

Give to the Lord glory, you heavens;
give to the Lord glory and power.
Give to the Lord glory due his Name;
worship the Lord in his holy courts.

The God of glory thunders!
The Lord hews flames of fire!

The voice of the Lord is over the waters,
the Lord over the sea waters.
The voice of the Lord in might;
the voice of the Lord in splendor.

The God of glory thunders!
The Lord hews flames of fire!

The voice of the Lord shatters the cedar trees;
  the Lord shatters the cedars of Lebanon.
The voice of the Lord makes Lebanon skip
    like a calf,
  and Sirion like a young wild ox.

  The God of glory thunders!
  The Lord hews flames of fire!

The voice of the Lord shakes the desert,
  the Lord shakes the desert of Kadesh.
The voice of the Lord makes the oak trees
    writhe,
  and strips the forests bare.

Everyone in his temple shouts:
  Glory! Glory!

The Lord is enthroned above the waters;
  the Lord is enthroned King for evermore.

The Lord gives strength to his people;
  the Lord blesses his people with peace.

Glory to the Father, and to the Son, and to
    the Holy Spirit:
  as it was in the beginning, is now, and will
    be for ever.   Amen.

Ant. From heaven came a sound of rushing
wind, and there appeared to them
fiery tongues.

Psalm Prayer

God of glory and majesty,
pour out your Spirit upon us
like a rushing wind and a flaming fire.
Give us the strength to do your will
and the peace that passes all understanding.
We ask this through Christ our Lord.
—Amen.

Reading   *Romans 8:9–11*

Live as the Spirit tells you to—if, in fact, God's
Spirit lives in you. Whoever does not have the
Spirit of Christ does not belong to him. But if
Christ lives in you, although your bodies are
going to die because of sin, yet the Spirit is life
for you because you have been put right with
God. If the Spirit of God, who raised Jesus
from death, lives in you, then he who raised
Christ from death will also give life to your
mortal bodies by the presence of his Spirit in
you.

Response

When the Spirit of truth comes,
—He will lead you into all truth.

Canticle of Mary   See page 101

Ant. Come, Holy Spirit, fill the hearts of your
faithful, and kindle in them the fire
of your love, alleluia.

Collect Prayer

Father,
you taught the hearts of your faithful people
by sending them the light of your Holy
Spirit.
In that Spirit give us right judgment
and the joy of his comfort and guidance.
We make our prayer through Jesus Christ our
Lord.
—Amen.

Blessing

May the blessing of almighty God, the
Father, + the Son and the Holy Spirit,
descend upon us and remain with us
always.
—Amen.

Tuesday—All Saints

MORNING

O Lord, + open my lips.
—And my mouth will proclaim your praise.

Psalm 24[a]   The Saints in the Presence of
God

Ant. Blessed are the pure in heart: they shall
see God.

The world and all that is in it belong to the
Lord;
the earth and all who live on it are his.
He built it on the deep waters beneath the
earth
and laid its foundations in the ocean
depths.

Who has the right to go up the Lord's hill?
Who is allowed to enter his holy temple?
He who is pure in act and in thought,
who does not worship idols,
or make false promises.

The Lord will bless him;
   God his Savior will declare him innocent.
Such are the people who come to God,
   who come into the presence of the God of
      Jacob.

Glory to the Father, and to the Son, and to
      the Holy Spirit:
   as it was in the beginning, is now, and will
      be for ever.   Amen.

Ant. Blessed are the pure in heart: they shall
      see God.

Psalm Prayer

God of all holiness,
you are glorified in the assembly of the
      saints,
and in crowning their merits
you are but crowning your own gifts.
Surrounded by such a crowd of witnesses,
help us run our appointed race
and with them receive a never-fading garland
      of glory,
through Jesus Christ our Lord.
—Amen.

Reading   *Micah 6:8*

This is what the Lord asks of you: only this, to
    act justly,
to love tenderly and to walk humbly with your
    God.

Response

The righteous shall praise your name, O
    Lord.
—The upright shall walk in your presence.

Canticle of Zachary   See page 94.

Ant. The just will shine like the sun in their
      Father's kingdom.

Collect Prayer

Almighty and ever-living God,
you kindled the flame of love
in the hearts of your saints.
Give us the same power of faith and love
that, as we rejoice in their triumphs,
we may profit by their example and their
    prayers.
We ask this through Christ our Lord.
—Amen.

Blessing

May Christ, the King of glory, + grant us his
    peace.
—Amen.

NOON

How wonderful is God in all his saints!
—Come, let us adore the Holy One.

Reading

In the earthly liturgy, by way of foretaste, we
share in that heavenly liturgy which is celebrated in the holy city of Jerusalem toward
which we journey as pilgrims, and in which
Christ is sitting at the right hand of God, a
minister of the sanctuary and of the true
tabernacle; we sing a hymn to the Lord's glory
with all the warriors of the heavenly army;
venerating the memory of the saints, we hope
for some part and fellowship with them; we
eagerly await the Savior, our Lord Jesus
Christ, until he, our life, shall appear and we
too will appear with him in glory.

Constitution on the Sacred Liturgy, 8

Response

You, Christ, are the king of glory,
  the eternal Son of the Father.
When you became man to set us free
  you did not spurn the Virgin's womb.
You overcame the sting of death,
  and opened the kingdom of heaven to all
    believers.
You are seated at God's right hand in glory.
  We believe that you will come, and be our
    judge.
Come then, Lord, and help your people,
  bought with the price of your own blood,
And bring us with your saints
  to glory everlasting.

Te Deum Laudamus

Prayer

May all your saints, O Lord,
come to our aid in every time and place
that, while we recall their meritorious lives,
we may experience the help of their prayers.
Grant peace in our time,
purge your Church of every evil,
direct our hearts according to your will,
reward those who do us good,
and grant eternal rest to all the faithful
    departed;
through Jesus Christ our Lord.
—Amen.

EVENING

O God, + come to my assistance.
—O Lord, make haste to help me.

Psalm 145   One Universal Act of Praise

Ant. Worship the Lord in the beauty of
          holiness.

I will exalt you, O God my King,
    and bless your Name for ever and ever.
Day after day will I bless you,
    and praise your Name for ever and ever.

Great is the Lord and worthy of great praise;
    there is no limit to his greatness.
Age to age praises your works,
    and proclaims your mighty deeds.
They ponder the splendor and glory of your
          majesty,
    and all your marvelous wonders.
They will relate your awesome acts,
    and recount your greatness.
They will call to remembrance your great
          goodness,
    and sing out with joy your righteousness.

The Lord is gracious and merciful,
  slow to anger and steadfast in love.
The Lord is good to everyone;
  his compassion reaches all whom he has
    made.
All your creation praises you, O Lord;
  all your faithful people bless you.
They proclaim the glory of your kingdom,
  and tell of all your power;
That everyone may know of your might,
  and the glorious splendor of your
    kingdom.

Glory to the Father, and to the Son, and to the
    Holy Spirit:
as it was in the beginning, is now, and will be
    for ever.   Amen.

Ant. Worship the Lord in the beauty of
         holiness.

Psalm Prayer

Heavenly Father,
as we rejoice with the holy men and women
of every age and race,
may we receive from you
the fullness of forgiveness
we have always desired.
Please grant this through Christ our Lord.
—Amen.

Reading   *Revelation 7:9–10*

I looked and there was an enormous crowd—
no one could count all the people! They were
from every race, tribe, nation, and language,
and they stood in front of the throne and of
the Lamb, dressed in white robes and holding
palm branches in their hands. They called out
in a loud voice: "Salvation comes from our
God, who sits on the throne, and from the
Lamb!"

Response

Let God's people rejoice in their triumph.
—And sing joyfully at their feasts.

Canticle of Mary   See page 101.

Ant. The whole company of heaven
        proclaims your glory,
        O Blessed Trinity, one God.

Collect Prayer

Almighty and ever-living God,
by your grace
we live in communion with all your saints.

By their prayers
make us true disciples of your Son
during our earthly pilgrimage,
and in our heavenly home
let us share their fullness of joy,
through Jesus Christ our Lord.
—Amen.

Blessing

May Jesus Christ, the Lord of all saints, +
    bless us and keep us.
—Amen.

Tuesday—The Faithful Departed

MORNING

O Lord, + open my lips.
—And my mouth will proclaim your praise.

Psalm 27[a]   A Song of Confidence in God's
Unfailing Help

Ant. I will sing, I will praise the Lord!

The Lord is my light and my salvation;
 I will fear no one.
The Lord protects me from all danger;
 I will not be afraid.

When evil men attack me and try to kill me,
 they stumble and fall.
Even if a whole army surrounds me,
 I will not be afraid;
even if my enemies attack me,
 I will still trust God.

I have asked the Lord for one thing;
   one thing only do I want:
to live in the Lord's house all my life,
   to marvel at his goodness,
   and to ask his guidance there.

In times of trouble he will protect me in his
      shelter;
   he will keep me safe in his temple,
   and place me securely on a high rock.

With shouts of joy I will offer sacrifices in his
      temple;
   I will sing, I will praise the Lord!

Give them eternal rest, O Lord,
   and may your light shine on them for ever.

Ant. I will sing, I will praise the Lord!

Psalm Prayer

Father of Jesus, our risen Lord,
be our light and our salvation,
keep us safe in your temple
and enable us to praise you,
now and for ever.
—Amen

Reading   *Wisdom 1:13–14*

God did not make death, nor does he rejoice in the destruction of the living. For he fashioned all things that they might have being and the creatures of the world are wholesome.

Response

Holy is God, holy and mighty,
—Holy and living for ever.

Canticle of Zachary   See page 94.

Ant. I am the resurrection and the life.
        Whoever believes in me will live,
        even though he dies;
        and whoever lives and believes in me
        will never die, alleluia.

Collect Prayer

God, our Creator and Redeemer,
by your power Christ conquered death
and returned to you in glory.
May all your people who have gone before us
        in faith
share his victory
and enjoy the vision of your glory for ever.
We make our prayer through Jesus our Lord.
—Amen.

For one person:

Almighty God, our Father,
we firmly believe that your Son died and rose
    to life.
We pray for our brother (sister) N.,
who has died in Christ.
Raise him (her) at the last day
to share the glory of the risen Christ,
who lives and reigns with you and the Holy
    Spirit,
one God, for ever and ever.
—Amen.

For an anniversary:

God of mercy,
we keep this anniversary
of the death (burial) of N. our brother (sister).
Give him (her) light, happiness and peace.
We ask this through Christ our Lord.
—Amen.

Blessing

May the souls of the faithful departed
    through the mercy of God
    rest in peace.
—Amen.

NOON

Come, let us worship the Lord.
—All things live for him.

Reading   *1 Corinthians 15:20–24*

Christ has been raised from death, as the
guarantee that those who sleep in death will
also be raised. For just as death came by
means of a man, in the same way the rising
from death comes by means of a man. For just
as all die because of their union to Adam, in
the same way all will be raised to life because
of their union to Christ. But each one in his
own proper order: Christ, the first of all; then
those who belong to Christ, at the time of his
coming.

Response   Psalm 23

The Lord is my shepherd;
    there is nothing I shall want.
Fresh and green are the pastures
    where he gives me repose.
Near restful waters he leads me,
    to revive my drooping spirit.

He guides me along the right path;
    he is true to his name.
If I should walk in the valley of darkness
    no evil would I fear.
You are there with your crook and your staff;
    with these you give me comfort.

You have prepared a banquet for me
    in the sight of my foes.
My head you have anointed with oil;
    my cup is overflowing.
Surely goodness and kindness shall follow
    me
    all the days of my life.
In the Lord's own house shall I dwell
    for ever and ever.   *Grail*

Give them eternal rest, O Lord,
    and may your light shine on them for ever.

Prayer

Lord Jesus Christ, shepherd of your Church,
you give us new birth in the waters of
    baptism,
anoint us with saving oil,
and call us to salvation at your table.
Dispel the terrors of death
and the darkness of error.
Lead your people along safe paths
that they may rest securely in you

and live for ever in your Father's house,
 where you reign for ever and ever.
—Amen.

EVENING

O God, + come to my assistance.
—O Lord, make haste to help me.

Psalm 130.   A Plea for Mercy and
             Forgiveness

Ant. If you kept a record of our sins, who
          could escape being condemned?

In my despair I call to you, Lord.
   Hear my cry, Lord,
   listen to my call for help!
If you kept a record of our sins,
   who could escape being condemned?
But you forgive us,
   so that we should fear you.

I wait eagerly for the Lord's help,
   and in his word I trust.
I wait for the Lord,
   more eagerly than watchmen wait for the
      dawn,
than watchmen wait for the dawn.

Israel, trust in the Lord,
  because his love is constant,
  and he is always willing to save.
He will save his people Israel
  from all their sins.

Give them eternal rest, O Lord,
  and may your light shine on them for ever.

Ant. If you kept a record of our sins, who
        could escape being condemned?

Psalm Prayer

God of love,
have mercy on our brothers and sisters who
    have died.
May their faith and hope in you be rewarded
    by eternal life.
We ask this through Christ our Lord.
—Amen.

Reading   *1 Thessalonians 4:13–14*

Brothers and sisters, we want you to know the
truth about those who have died, so that you
will not be sad, as are those who have no
hope. We believe that Jesus died and rose
again; so we believe that God will bring with
Jesus those who have died believing in him.

Response

Heaven is our home.
—And we eagerly await the coming of our
    Savior.

Canticle of Mary   See page 101.

Ant. I am the bread of life. Anyone who eats
    this bread will live for ever.

Collect Prayer

Father,
source of forgiveness and salvation for all,
hear our prayer.
By the prayers of the ever-virgin Mary,
may our friends, relatives, and benefactors
who have gone from this world
come to share eternal happiness with all your
    saints.
Please grant this through Christ our Lord.
—Amen.

*Or one of the collects provided at Morning Prayer,
    pages 125–126.*

Blessing

May Christ Jesus, the Son of the living God,
    bless + us and keep us.
—Amen.

Wednesday—St. Joseph, the Husband of Mary

MORNING

O Lord, + open my lips.
—And my mouth will proclaim your praise.

Psalm 92 God's Upright Servant
Sings a Song of Praise

Ant. Joseph was a man who always did what
was right (Mt 1:19).

How good it is to give thanks to the Lord,
  to sing in your honor, Most High God,
to proclaim your constant love every morning,
  and your faithfulness every night,
with the music of stringed instruments,
  and with melody on the harp.
Your mighty acts, Lord, make me glad;
  because of what you have done
    I sing for joy.

How great are your acts, Lord!
How deep are your thoughts!
Here is something a fool cannot know,
a stupid man cannot understand:
the wicked may grow like weeds,
and all evildoers may prosper;
yet they will be totally destroyed,
because you, Lord, are supreme for ever.

The righteous will flourish like palm trees;
they will grow like the cedars of Lebanon.
They are like trees planted in the house of the Lord,
that flourish in the temple of our God,
that still bear fruit in old age,
and are always green and strong.
This shows that the Lord is just;
in him, my defender, there is no wrong.

Glory to the Father, and to the Son, and to the
Holy Spirit:
as it was in the beginning, is now, and will be
for ever. Amen.

Ant. Joseph was a man who
always did what was right.

Psalm Prayer

Father,
you entrusted our Savior to the care of St.
    Joseph.
By the help of his prayers
may your Church continue to serve its Lord,
    Jesus Christ,
who lives with you and the Holy Spirit,
one God, for ever and ever.
—Amen.

Reading   *Sirach 26:1-4*

Happy the husband of a good wife; twice-
lengthened are his days. A worthy wife brings
joy to her husband; peaceful and full is his life.
A good wife is a generous gift bestowed upon
him who fears the Lord; be he rich or poor, his
heart is content, and a smile is ever on his
face.

Response

Mary was promised in marriage to a man
    named Joseph,
—Who was a descendant of King David.

Canticle of Zachary   See page 94.

Ant. Joseph was a faithful and wise steward
        whom the Lord set over his family.

Collect Prayer

God,
in your infinite wisdom and love
you chose Joseph to be the husband of Mary,
the mother of your Son.
May we who enjoy his protection on earth
have his prayers to help us to heaven.
We ask this through Christ our Lord.
—Amen.

Blessing

May the Word made flesh, full of grace and
    truth, + bless and keep us.
—Amen.

NOON

Let us praise Christ the Lord,
—As we celebrate the memory of St. Joseph.

Reading

I took for my advocate and lord the glorious St. Joseph and commended myself earnestly to him; and I found that this my father and lord delivered me both from this trouble [paralysis] and also from other and greater troubles.... I do not remember even now that I have ever asked anything of him which he has failed to grant. I am astonished at the great favors which God has bestowed on me through this blessed saint, and at the perils from which he has freed me, both in body and in soul. To other saints the Lord seems to have given grace to succor us in some of our necessities but of this glorious saint my experience is that he succors us in them all.... I have never known anyone to be truly devoted to him and render him particular services who did not notably advance in virtue, for he gives very real help to souls who commend themselves to him.... Those who practice prayer should have a special affection for him always. I do not know how any one can think of the Queen of the Angels, during the time that she suffered so much with the Child Jesus, without giving thanks to St. Joseph for the way he helped them. If anyone cannot find a master to teach him how to pray, let him take this glorious saint as his master and he will not go astray.

St. Teresa of Avila (1515–1582)
Autobiography, 6

Response   *Psalm 89:1–4, 26–28*

Lord, I will always sing of your constant love;
    at all times I will proclaim your
        faithfulness.
I know that your love will last for ever,
    that your faithfulness is as permanent as
        the sky.

You said, "I have made a covenant with the
        man I chose;
    I have promised my servant David,
'A descendant of yours will always be king;
    I will preserve your kingdom for ever.'"

He will say to me,
    'You are my father and my God;
    you are my protector and Savior.'
I will make him my firstborn son,
    the greatest of all kings.
I will always keep my promise to him,
    and my covenant with him will last for
        ever.

Prayer

Good St. Joseph,
ever-watchful guardian of the holy family,
protect the chosen people of Jesus Christ,
keep us free from the blight of error and
    corruption,
and be our ally in the conflict with the
    powers of darkness.
As of old you rescued the child Jesus from
    the plots of Herod,
so now defend the universal Church from all
    harm.
Keep us one and all under your continual
    protection,
so that by your help and example,
we may lead a holy life,
die a godly death,
and attain to a happy eternity in heaven.
—Amen.

EVENING

O God, + come to my assistance.
—O Lord, make haste to help me.

Psalm 1   The Lord Preserves His Saints

Ant. The father and mother of Jesus
        marvelled at what was being said
        about him.

Blessed are they
　who do not follow the advice of the
　　wicked,
nor take their stance in the way of sinners,
　nor seat themselves in the company of
　　scoffers.

Their delight is in the law of the Lord,
　and in his law they meditate day and
　　night.
They are like a tree planted by water-brooks
　that bears its fruit in season,
　with leaves that never wither.
In everything they do,
　they prosper.

Not so with the wicked!
　They are like chaff blown away by the
　　wind;
they will not rise up in the judgment,
　nor will sinners in the company of the just.
For the Lord knows the way of the just;
　but the way of the wicked will perish.

Glory to the Father, and to the Son, and to
　　the Holy Spirit:
as it was in the beginning, is now, and will
　be for ever.　　Amen.

Ant. The father and mother of Jesus
　　　　marvelled at what was being said
　　　　about him.

Psalm Prayer

God our Father,
Creator and Ruler of the universe,
in every age you call us
to develop and use our gifts for the good of
        others.
With St. Joseph as our example and guide,
help us to do the work you have asked
and come to the rewards you have promised.
Please grant this through Christ our Lord.
—Amen.

Reading   *Colossians 3:23–24*

Whatever you do, work at it with all your
heart, as though you were working for the
Lord, and not for men. Remember that the
Lord will reward you; you will receive what he
has kept for his people. For Christ is the real
Master you serve.

Response

Well done, good and faithful servant!
—Come and share my happiness.

Canticle of Mary   See page 101.

Ant. Unfading will be his memory. Through
        all generations his name will live.

Collect Prayer

Heavenly Father,
from the family of your servant David
you raised up Joseph to be the guardian of
    your incarnate Son
and the spouse of his virgin mother.
Give us grace to imitate his uprightness of
    life
and his obedience to your commands,
through Jesus Christ our Lord.
—Amen.

Blessing

May Jesus, our incarnate God, + bless and
    keep us.
—Amen.

The language that God hears best is the silent
    language of love.

St. John of the Cross

Thursday—The Blessed Sacrament

MORNING

O Lord, + open my lips.
—And my mouth will proclaim your praise.

Psalm 84   The Place of His Presence

Ant. I will go to the altar of God, the God of
        my joy.

How I love your temple, Almighty God!
    How I want to be there!
I long for the courts of the Lord's temple.
    With my whole being I sing with joy to the
        living God.

Even the sparrows have built a nest,
    and the swallows have their own home;
they keep their young near your altars,
    Lord Almighty, my king and my God.
How happy are those who live in your
        temple,
    always singing praise to you!

How happy are those whose strength comes
    from you,
    who are eager to make the pilgrimage to
    Mount Zion.
As they pass through the dry valley
    it becomes a place of springs;
    the early rain fills it with pools.
They grow stronger as they go;
    they will see the God of gods on Zion!

Hear my prayer, Lord God Almighty;
    listen, God of Jacob!
Bless our king, God,
    the king you have chosen!

One day spent in your temple
    is better than a thousand anywhere else;
I would rather stand at the gate of the house
    of my God
    than live in the homes of the wicked.

Glory to the Father, and to the Son, and to
    the Holy Spirit:
    as it was in the beginning, is now, and will
    be for ever.   Amen.

Ant. I will go to the altar of God, the God of
    my joy.

Psalm Prayer

God of presence, God of power,
refresh and strengthen us with the bread of
    life
that we may eagerly continue our pilgrimage
and grow stronger as we travel toward our
    heavenly home.
We ask this through Christ our Lord.
—Amen.

Reading   *Malachi 1:11*

From the rising of the sun, even to its setting,
my name is great among the nations; and
everywhere they bring sacrifice to my name,
and a pure offering; for great is my name
among the nations, says the Lord of hosts.

Response

Come and eat my bread.
—Drink the wine I have prepared.

Canticle of Zachary   See page 94.

Ant. I am the living bread that came down
        from heaven. If anyone eats this
        bread he will live for ever.

144

Collect Prayer

Lord Jesus Christ,
you gave us the Eucharist
as the memorial of your suffering and death.
May our worship of this sacrament of your
    body and blood
help us to know the salvation you won for us
and the peace of the kingdom
where you live with the Father and the Holy
    Spirit,
one God, for ever and ever.
—Amen.

Blessing

May Christ, the bread of life, + be our
    strength and stay.
—Amen.

NOON

Come, let us adore Christ the Lord, the bread
    of life.
—Come, let us adore him.

Reading

It was to impress the vastness of his love more
firmly on the hearts of the faithful that our
Lord instituted this sacrament at the Last
Supper. As he was on the point of leaving the
world to go to the Father, after celebrating the
Passover with his disciples, he left it as a perpetual memorial of his passion. It was the fulfillment of the ancient figures and the greatest
of all his miracles, while for those who were to
experience the sorrow of his departure, it was
destined to be a unique and abiding consolation.

St. Thomas Aquinas (1225–1274),
Opusculum 57, 4.

Response

Hail our Savior's glorious Body,
Which his Virgin Mother bore;
Hail the Blood which, shed for sinners,
Did a broken world restore;
Hail the sacrament most holy,
Flesh and Blood of Christ adore!

Come, adore this wondrous presence;
Bow to Christ, the source of grace!
Here is kept the ancient promise
Of God's earthly dwelling place!
Sight is blind before God's glory,
Faith alone may see his face!

Glory be to God the Father,
Praise to his co-equal Son,
Adoration to the Spirit,
Bond of love, in Godhead one!
Blest be God by all creation
Joyously while ages run.

Prayer *Pange Lingua Gloriosi*

Lord Jesus Christ,
we worship you living among us
in the sacrament of your body and blood.
Be for us in the Eucharist
strength to live the mystery of your presence.
May we offer to your Father in heaven
the broken bread of undivided love.
May we offer to our brothers and sisters
a life poured out in loving service of that
      kingdom
where you live with the Father and the Holy
      Spirit,
one God, for ever and ever.
—Amen.

EVENING

O God, + come to my assistance.
—O Lord, make haste to help me.

Psalm 111   A Memorial Meal of God's
Wonderful Actions

Ant. Our kind and merciful Lord never
forgets his covenant, alleluia.

With all my heart I will thank the Lord,
in the meeting of his people.
How wonderful are the things the Lord does!
All who are pleased with them want to
understand them.
All he does is full of honor and majesty;
his righteousness is eternal.

The Lord does not let us forget his wonderful
actions;
he is kind and merciful.
He provides food for those who fear him;
he never forgets his covenant.
He has shown his power to his people,
by giving them the lands of foreigners.

In all he does he is faithful and just;
all his commandments are dependable.
They last for all time;
they were given in truth and
righteousness.

He brought salvation to his people,
  and made an eternal covenant with them.
  Holy and mighty is he!

The way to become wise is to fear the Lord;
  he gives sound judgment to all who obey
    his commands.
  He is to be praised for ever!

Glory to the Father, and to the Son, and to
    the Holy Spirit:
  as it was in the beginning, is now, and will
    be for ever. Amen.

Ant. Our kind and merciful Lord never
      forgets his covenant, alleluia.

Psalm Prayer

Kind and merciful Lord,
in the wonderful sacrament of the altar
you give us a living memorial of your dying
    and rising
and of the everlasting covenant established in
    your blood.
Keep us ever mindful of your wonderful
    actions
and faithful to your dependable
    commandments.
You live and reign for ever and ever.
—Amen.

Reading   *1 Corinthians 10:16–17*

The cup of blessing for which we give thanks
to God: do we not share in the blood of Christ
when we drink from this cup? And the bread
we break: do we not share in the body of
Christ when we eat this bread? Because there
is the one bread, all of us, though many, are
one body, because we all share the same loaf.

Response

The Lord gave them bread from heaven.
—Sending down manna for them to eat.

Canticle of Mary   See page 101.

Ant. How sacred is the feast
in which Christ is our food,
the memorial of his passion is
celebrated anew,
our hearts are filled with grace,
and we are given a pledge of the glory
which is to come, alleluia.

Collect Prayer

Father,
for your glory and our salvation
you appointed Jesus Christ eternal High
Priest.
May the people he gained for you by his
blood

come to share in the power of his cross and
resurrection
by celebrating his memorial in the Eucharist,
for he lives and reigns with you and the Holy
Spirit,
one God, for ever and ever.
—Amen.

Blessing

May Christ Jesus, Son of God and Son of
Mary, + bless and keep us.
—Amen.

Friday—The Holy Cross

MORNING

O Lord, + open my lips.
—And my mouth will proclaim your praise.

Psalm 2   Jesus Is God's Anointed and
                 Victorious Son

Ant. Behold the Lord's cross! Take flight, you
        hostile powers!
        Jesus is the conquering lion of the
        tribe of Judah.

Why do the nations plan rebellion?
  Why do these people make useless plots?
Their kings revolt,
  their rulers plot together
  against the Lord and his chosen king.
"Let us free ourselves from their rule," they
    say;
  "let us throw off their control."

From his throne in heaven the Lord laughs
    and makes fun of them.
He speaks to them in anger,
    and terrifies them with his fury.
"On Zion, my sacred hill," he says,
    "I have installed my king."

"I will announce what the Lord declared,"
        says the king.
    "The Lord said to me: 'You are my Son;
today I have become your Father.

Ask, and I will give you all the nations;
    the whole earth will be yours.
You will rule over them with an iron hand;
    you will break them in pieces like a clay
        pot.'"

Now listen to me, you kings;
    pay attention, you rulers!
Serve the Lord with fear;
    tremble and bow down to him.

Glory to the Father, and to the Son, and to
    the Holy Spirit:
    as it was in the beginning, is now, and will
    be for ever. Amen.

Ant. Behold the Lord's cross! Take flight, you
        hostile powers!
        Jesus is the conquering lion of the
        tribe of Judah.

Psalm Prayer

Blessed be the cross of our Lord Jesus Christ,
for in him is our salvation, life and
    resurrection.
By the power of the cross, O Lord,
set us free from all our sins,
save us in the time of trial,
and raise us up on the great and final day.
You live and reign for ever and ever.
—Amen.

Reading
Hebrews 2:9–10

We see Jesus crowned with glory and honor now because of the death he suffered. It was only right that God, who creates and preserves all things, should make Jesus perfect through suffering, in order to bring many sons and daughters to share his glory. For Jesus is the one who leads them to salvation.

Response

We adore you, O Christ, and we bless you.
—For by your holy cross you have redeemed
    the world.

Canticle of Zachary   See page 94.

Ant. Christ is victor; Christ is ruler; Christ is
    Lord of all.

Collect Prayer

Lord Jesus Christ, suffering servant of God,
for our salvation
you were unjustly condemned to death,
mocked, scourged, and crowned with thorns,
pierced by nails and scorned by unbelievers.
By your holy and glorious wounds
guard us and keep us from all evil
and bring us to the victory you have won for
us.
You live and reign for ever and ever.
—Amen.

Blessing

May the glorious passion of our Lord Jesus
Christ + bring us to the joys of
paradise.
—Amen.

NOON

Come, let us worship Christ our Lord and
   Master.
—He was lifted up on the cross for our
   salvation.

Reading

The precious blood of our Lord Jesus Christ,
as truly as it is most precious, so truly is it
most plentiful. Behold and see the power of
this precious plenty of his precious blood. It
descended into hell and broke its bonds, and
delivered all who were there and who belong
to the court of heaven. The precious plenty of
his precious blood overflows all the earth, and
it is ready to wash from their sins all creatures
who are, have been and will be of good will.
The precious plenty of his precious blood ascended into heaven in the blessed body of our
Lord Jesus Christ, and it is flowing there in
him, praying to the Father for us, and this is
and will be so long as we have need. And
furthermore, it flows in all heaven, rejoicing in
the salvation of all who are and will be there,
and filling up the number which is lacking.

Julian of Norwich (1342–1416),
Showings, 12 (Long text)
156

Response

Moses prefigured the saving power of the
    cross,
  when he lifted up his staff
  and split the Red Sea in two,
  rescuing Israel on that day from the hand
    of Pharaoh (Ex 14).

Moses prefigured the saving power of the
    cross,
  when he cast a tree into Marah's bitter
    water,
  making them fresh and sweet for a thirsty
    people (Ex 15).

Moses prefigured the saving power of the
    cross,
  when Israel hardened its heart at Meribah
  and put God to the test at Massah in the
    desert.
  He struck the rock at Horeb with his staff
  and brought forth living waters to quench
    their thirst (Ex 17).

Moses prefigured the saving power of the
    cross,
  when he extended his arms in the form of a
    cross
  and defeated haughty Amalek in the desert
    of Sinai (Ex 17).

Moses prefigured the saving power of the
> cross,
>> when he laid twelve staffs down before the
>> Lord
>> in the tent of the commandments,
>> and Aaron's staff sprouted leaves,
>>> blossoms and ripe almonds (Num 17).

Moses prefigured the saving power of the
> cross,
>> when he made a serpent of bronze
>> and mounted it on a pole in the desert;
>> all who looked at it with faith
>> recovered from the serpents' sting (Num
>> 21).

Prayer

O Son of God and Savior of the world,
all these symbols now attain their perfection
and find their completion before our very
> eyes.
Reign from the noble tree of the cross
and establish the kingdom of God in our
> hearts,
You live and reign for ever and ever.
—Amen.

EVENING

O God, + come to my assistance.
—O Lord, make haste to help me.

Psalm 67 The Harvest of Christ's Voluntary
     Suffering

Ant. The holy cross shines in splendor. In the
    cross is victory. In the cross is
    power.

God, be merciful to us and bless us;
 look on us with kindness,
that the whole world may know your will;
 that all nations may know your salvation.

May the peoples praise you, God;
 may all peoples praise you!

May the nations be glad and sing for joy,
 because you judge the peoples with justice
 and guide all the nations.

May the peoples praise you, God;
 may all peoples praise you!

The land has produced its harvest;
 God, our God, has blessed us.
God has blessed us;
 may all people everywhere honor him.

May the peoples praise you, God;
  may all peoples praise you!

Glory to the Father, and to the Son, and to
    the Holy Spirit:
  as it was in the beginning, is now, and will
    be for ever.   Amen.
Ant. The holy cross shines in splendor. In the
          cross is victory. In the cross is
          power.

Psalm Prayer

Merciful Father,
look upon this family of yours
for which our Lord Jesus Christ
did not hesitate to hand himself over to
    sinners
and to undergo the torment of the cross;
he now lives and reigns with you and the
    Holy Spirit,
one God, for ever and ever.
—Amen.

Reading   *Galatians 2:20–21*

I have been put to death with Christ on his
cross, so that it is no longer I who live, but it is
Christ who lives in me. This life that I live
now, I live by faith in the Son of God, who
loved me and gave his life for me.

Response

The sign of the cross will appear in the
    heavens,
—When the Lord returns in glory.

Canticle of Mary   See page 101.

Ant. We worship you, Lord, we venerate
            your cross, we praise your
            resurrection.
        Through your cross you brought joy
        to the world.

Collect Prayer

Lord Jesus Christ, God's Son of heaven,
set your passion, your cross and your death
between your judgment and our souls,
now and in the hour of our death.
In your goodness
grant mercy and grace to the living
and forgiveness and rest to the dead;
to the Church and to the nation peace and
    concord;
and to us sinners life and glory without end.
You live and reign for ever and ever.
—Amen.

Blessing

By the standard of the cross, O Lord, +
    deliver us from all sin and danger.
—Amen.

Friday—The Sacred Heart of Jesus

MORNING

O Lord, + open my lips.
—And my mouth will proclaim your praise.

Psalm 36^b The Goodness of God Our Savior

Ant. I have come to set fire on the earth.
How I wish it were already aflame!

Lord, your constant love reaches the
heavens,
your faithfulness extends to the skies.
Your righteousness is firm like the great
mountains,
your judgments are like the depths of the
sea.
You, Lord, care for human beings and for
animals.

How precious, God, is your constant love!
  Humans find protection under the shadow
    of your wings.
They feast on the abundant food from your
      house;
  you give them to drink from the river of
    your goodness.
You are the source of all life,
  and because of your light we see the light.

Continue to love those who know you
  and to do good to those who are righteous.
Do not let the proud attack me
  or the wicked make me run away.

Glory to the Father, and to the Son, and to
    the Holy Spirit:
  as it was in the beginning, is now, and will
    be for ever.   Amen

Ant. I have come to set fire on the earth.
        How I wish it were already aflame!

Psalm Prayer

Lord Jesus, living flame of love,
protect us under the wings of your cross
and be our constant source of light and life.
You live and reign for ever and ever.
—Amen.

Reading *Ephesians 2:4–7*

God's mercy is so abundant, and his love for us is so great, that while we were spiritually dead in our disobedience, he brought us to life in Christ. It is by God's grace that you have been saved. In our union with Christ Jesus he raised us up with him to rule with him in the heavenly world. He did this to demonstrate for all time to come the extraordinary greatness of his grace in the love he showed us in Christ Jesus.

Response

Jesus is the Lamb of God.
—He takes away the sins of the world.

Canticle of Zachary See page 94.

Ant. With tender compassion our God has come to his people and set them free.

Collect Prayer

Father,
we rejoice in the gifts of love
we have received from the heart of Jesus your
  Son.
Open our hearts to share his life
and continue to bless us with his love.
We ask this through Christ our Lord.
—Amen.

Blessing

May the Heart of Jesus + be our light and our
    peace.
—Amen.

NOON

Come, let us worship Jesus.
—Whose heart was wounded for love of us.

Reading

Very merrily and gladly our Lord looked into
his side, and he gazed and said this: See how I
loved you; as if he had said: My child, if you
cannot look on my divinity, see here how I
suffered my side to be opened and my heart to
be split in two and to send out blood and
water, all that was in it; and this is a delight to
me, and I wish it to be so for you. Our Lord
showed this to me to make us glad and merry.

Julian of Norwich (1342–1416),
Showings, *13*

Response   *Psalm 103*

R/ His goodness endures for all generations.

Praise the Lord, my soul!
    All my being, praise his holy name!
Praise the Lord, my soul,
    and do not forget how kind he is.

R/ His goodness endures for all generations.

He forgives all my sins
and heals all my diseases;
he saves me from the grave
and blesses me with love and mercy;
he fills my life with good things,
so that I stay young and strong like an
eagle.

R/ His goodness endures for all generations.

The Lord is merciful and loving,
slow to become angry, and full of constant
love.
As high as the sky is above the earth,
so great is his love for those who fear him.

R/ His goodness endures for all generations.

As far as the east is from the west,
so far does he remove our sins from us.
As kind as a father is to his children,
so the Lord is kind to those who fear him.

R/ His goodness endures for all generations.

The Lord's love for those
    who honor him lasts for ever,
  and his goodness endures for all
    generations,
to those who are true to his covenant,
  and who faithfully obey his
    commandments.

R/ His goodness endures for all generations.

Prayer

May the Heart of Jesus
in the most Blessed Sacrament
be praised, adored and loved,
with grateful affection,
at every moment,
in all the tabernacles of the world,
even unto the end of time.

EVENING

O God, + come to my assistance.
—O Lord, make haste to help me.

Psalm 98   Jesus Is the King of All Hearts

Ant. The plans of Christ's heart endure from
       age to age.

Sing a new song to the Lord;
  he has done wonderful things!
By his own power and holy strength
  he has won the victory.
The Lord announced his victory;
  he made his saving power known to the
    nations.
He kept his promise to the people of Israel
  with constant love and loyalty for them.
All people everywhere
  have seen the victory of our God.

Sing for joy to the Lord, all the earth;
  praise him with songs and shouts of joy!
Sing praises to the Lord with harps;
  play music on the harps!
With trumpets and horns,
  shout for joy before the Lord, the King!

Roar, sea, and all creatures in you;
  sing, earth, and all who live there!
Clap your hands, oceans;
  hills, sing together with joy before the
    Lord,
  because he comes to rule the earth!
He will rule all peoples of the world
  with justice and fairness.

Glory to the Father, and to the Son, and to
  the Holy Spirit:

as it was in the beginning, is now, and will
be for ever. Amen.

Ant. The plans of Christ's heart endure from
age to age.

Psalm Prayer

Lord our God,
open our hearts to the gentle rule of your
Son,
our eternal priest and universal king.
May his kingdom of justice, peace and love
establish its dominion everywhere.
We ask this through Jesus the Lord.
—Amen.

Reading   *Romans 8:38–39*

I am certain that nothing can separate us from
Christ's love: neither death nor life; neither
angels nor other heavenly rulers or powers;
neither the present nor the future; neither the
world above nor the world below—there is
nothing in all creation that will ever be able to
separate us from the love of God which is ours
through Christ Jesus our Lord.

Response

My yoke is easy, says the Lord.
—My burden is light.

Canticle of Mary   See page 101.

Ant. One of the soldiers plunged his spear
into Jesus' side,
and at once blood and water poured
out.

Collect Prayer

Father,
we honor the heart of your Son
broken by our cruelty,
yet symbol of love's triumph,
pledge of all that we can be.
Teach us to see Christ in the lives we touch,
to offer him living worship
by love-filled service to our brothers and
sisters.
We ask this through Christ our Lord.
—Amen.

Blessing

May the Heart of Jesus + be our life and our
salvation.
—Amen.

Saturday—The Blessed Virgin Mary

MORNING

O Lord, + open my lips.
—And my mouth will proclaim your praise.

Psalm 46   Mary Is the Holy Place in Which God Dwells

Ant. He shall be called Emmanuel:
     God-is-with-us (Mt 1:23).

God is our shelter and strength,
  always ready to help in times of trouble.
So we will not be afraid, even if the earth is
    shaken
  and mountains fall into the ocean depths;
even if the seas roar and rage,
  and the hills are shaken by the violence.
The Lord Almighty is with us;
  the God of Jesus is our refuge!

There is a river that brings joy to the city of
      God,
  to the sacred house of the Most High.
God lives in the city, and it will never be
      destroyed;
  at early dawn he will come to its help.
Nations are terrified, kingdoms are shaken;
  God roars out and the earth dissolves.
The Lord Almighty is with us;
  the God of Jesus is our refuge!

Come, see what the Lord has done!
  See what amazing things he has done on
      earth!
He stops wars all over the world;
  he breaks bows, destroys spears,
  and sets shields on fire!
He says, "Stop your fighting and know that I
      am God,
  supreme among the nations, supreme over
      the world!"
The Lord Almighty is with us;
  the God of Jesus is our refuge!

Glory to the Father, and to the Son, and to
      the Holy Spirit:
  as it was in the beginning, is now, and will
      be forever. Amen.

Ant. He shall be called Emmanuel:
      God-is-with-us.

Psalm Prayer

God our Father,
you chose the Blessed Virgin Mary
to become the Mother of your Son our
    Savior;
grant that we who call to mind
her great faith and love
may in all things seek to do your will
and always rejoice in your salvation.
We ask this through Jesus Christ our Lord.
—Amen.

Reading   *Isaiah 7:10; 9:5–6*

The virgin shall be with child, and bear a son.
They name him Wonder-Counselor, God-
Hero, Father-Forever, Prince of Peace. His
dominion is vast and for ever peaceful, from
David's throne, and over his kingdom, which
he confirms and sustains by judgment and
justice, both now and for ever.

Response

The Word was made flesh, alleluia.
—And lived among us, alleluia.

Canticle of Zachary   See page 94.

Ant. Hail Mary, full of grace, the Lord is with
        you.

173

Collect Prayer

God our Father,
may we always have the prayers
of the Virgin Mother Mary,
for through Jesus Christ her Son
you bring us light and salvation;
he lives and reigns with you and the Holy
    Spirit,
one God, for ever and ever.
—Amen.

Seasonal Collect Prayers

Advent:

Father,
in your plan for our salvation
your Word became flesh,
announced by an angel and born of the
    Virgin Mary.
May we who believe that she is the Mother of
    God
receive the help of her prayers.
We ask this through Christ our Lord.

Christmastide:

Father,
you gave the human race eternal salvation
through the motherhood of the Virgin Mary.

May we experience the help of her prayers in
    our lives,
for through her we received the very source
    of life,
your Son, our Lord Jesus Christ,
who lives and reigns with you and the Holy
    Spirit,
one God, for ever and ever.

Lent:

Lord,
fill our hearts with your love,
and as you revealed to us by an angel
the coming of your Son as man,
so lead us through his suffering and death
to the glory of his resurrection,
for he lives and reigns with you and the Holy
    Spirit,
one God, for ever and ever.

Eastertide:

God our Father,
you give joy to the world
by the resurrection of your Son, our Lord
    Jesus Christ.
Through the prayers of his mother, the
    Virgin Mary,
bring us to the happiness of eternal life.
We ask this through Christ our Lord.

Blessing

May the Virgin Mary with her holy Child +
    bless and keep us.
—Amen.

NOON

Come, let us adore Christ, the Son of Mary.
—Come, let us adore the Word made flesh.

Reading

With the same joyful appearance our Lord
looked down on his right, and brought to
mind where our Lady stood at the time of his
Passion, and he said: Do you wish to see her?
And I answered and said: Yes, good Lord,
great thanks, if it be your will. And Jesus
showed me a spiritual vision of her. Just as
before I had seen her small and simple, now
he showed her high and noble and glorious
and more pleasing to him than all creatures.
And so he wishes it to be known that all who
take delight in him should take delight in her,
and in the delight that he has in her and she in
him.

Julian of Norwich (1342–1416), Showings, *13*

Response   *Luke 1:28; Judith 13:18–20: 15:9*

R/ Hail Mary, full of grace, the Lord is with
     you.

Blessed are you, daughter, by the Most High
     God,
   above all women on earth.

And blessed be the Lord God, the creator of
     heaven and earth,
   who guided your blow at the head of the
     chief of our enemies.

R/ Hail Mary, full of grace, the Lord is with
     you.

Your deed of hope will never be forgotten
   by those who tell of the might of God.

R/ Hail Mary, full of grace, the Lord is with
     you.

May God make this redound to your
     everlasting honor,
   rewarding you with blessings,
   because you averted our disaster,
   walking uprightly before our God.

R/ Hail Mary, full of grace, the Lord is with
     you.

You are the glory of Jerusalem,
   the surpassing joy of Israel.
   You are the splendid boast of our people.

R/ Hail Mary, full of grace, the Lord is with
     you.

Salutation to the Blessed Virgin Mary

Hail, holy Lady,
  most holy Queen,
  Mary, Mother of God,
  ever-virgin;
Chosen by the most holy Father in heaven,
  consecrated by him,
  with his most holy and beloved Son
  and the Holy Spirit, the Comforter.
On you descended and in you still remains
  all the fullness of grace
  and every good.
Hail, his palace.
Hail, his tabernacle.
Hail, his robe.
Hail, his handmaid.
Hail, his mother.
And hail, all holy virtues,
  who by the grace and inspiration of the
    Holy Spirit,
  are poured into the hearts of the faithful
  so that, faithless no longer,
  they may be faithful servants of God
  through you.

St. Francis of Assisi (1181–1226)

EVENING

O God, + come to my assistance.
—O Lord, make haste to help me.

Psalm 87   Mary Is God's City, the Mother of
All Nations

Ant. Wonderful things are said about you, O
holy Mother of God.

God built his city on the sacred hills;
  he loves the city of Jerusalem
  more than any other place in Israel.
Listen, city of God,
  to the wonderful things he says about you:

"When I list the nations that obey me,
  I will include Egypt and Babylonia;
and I will say of Philistia, Tyre, and Ethiopia,
  that they also belong to Jerusalem."

Of Zion it will be said
  that all nations belong there,
  and the Most High will make her strong.
The Lord will write a list of the peoples,
  and include them all as citizens of
    Jerusalem.
  All who live there will sing and dance.

Glory to the Father, and to the Son, and to
    the Holy Spirit:
  as it was in the beginning, is now, and will
    be for ever.   Amen.

Ant. Wonderful things are said about you, O
      holy Mother of God.

Psalm Prayer

Lord, may the prayers of the Virgin Mary
bring us protection from danger
and freedom from sin
that we may come to the joy of your peace.
We ask this through Christ our Lord.
—Amen.

Reading   *Revelation 21:1–3*

I, John, saw new heavens and a new earth.
The former heavens and the former earth had
passed away, and the sea was no longer. I also
saw a new Jerusalem, the holy city, coming
down out of heaven from God, beautiful as a
bride prepared to meet her husband. I heard a
loud voice from the throne cry out: "This is
God's dwelling among men. He shall dwell
with them and they shall be his people, and
he shall be their God who is always with
them."

Response

Blessed are you among women, alleluia.
—And blessed is the fruit of your womb,
    alleluia.

Canticle of Mary   See page 101.

Ant. We turn to you for protection,
        holy Mother of God.
    From your place in heaven
        help us in all our needs.
    Blessed Virgin in glory,
        save us from every danger.

Collect Prayer

Lord God,
give to your people the joy
of continual health in mind and body.
With the prayers of the Virgin Mary to help
        us,
guide us through the sorrows of this life
to eternal happiness in the life to come.
Please grant this through Christ our Lord.
—Amen.

*For the seasonal collects see above at Morning
    Prayer, 174–175.*

Blessing

May the Word made flesh, full of grace and
 truth, + bless and keep us.
—Amen.

4. The Year of Our Lord

ON THE LORD'S DAY each week, we celebrate the Paschal Mystery in word and sacrament; it is the "original feast day, the foundation and kernel of the whole liturgical year." (Vatican II)

Within the cycle of the year, we let the whole mystery of Christ unfold before us: incarnation, birth, death, resurrection, ascension, pentecost and parousia. By step-by-step meditation on the several facets of the one mystery, we can contemplate them more at leisure, lay hold of them more securely, and fill our spirit with their refreshing power.

The rich depths of the Mystery of Christ are presented to us in the poetry and prayer of our Catholic tradition. Each selection lends itself to prayer and meditation during the appropriate season.

All seasons are fruitful for Christians,
for all are full of Jesus Christ.

Bossuet (1627–1704)

Advent

Hymn

Comfort my people and quiet her fear;
Tell her the time of salvation draws near.
Tell her I come to remove all her shame;
"She that is pitied" shall be her new name.

Say to the cities of Judah: "Behold!
Gentle, yet mighty, the arm of the Lord
Rescues the captives of darkness and sin,
Bringing them justice and joy without end."

Mountains and hills shall become like a plain.
Vanished are mourning and hunger and
    pain;
Never again shall these war against you;
"See, he comes quickly to make all things
    new!"

St. Joseph's Abbey, 1967
Based on Isaiah 40

Psalm 24[b]   Christ Will Come Again in Glory

Fling wide the gates,
open the ancient doors,
and the king of glory will enter in!

Who is this great king of glory?

He is the Lord Christ, strong and mighty,
the Lord Jesus, victorious in battle.

Fling wide the gates,
open the ancient doors,
and the king of glory will enter in!

Who is this great king of glory?

He is our Lord Jesus Christ,
he is the Lord of hosts,
he is the great king of glory!

Psalm Prayer

All-powerful God,
increase our strength of will for doing good
that Christ may find an eager welcome at his
    coming
and call us to his side in the kingdom of
    heaven,
where he lives and reigns with you and the
    Holy Spirit,
one God, for ever and ever.
—Amen.

Canticle of Zephaniah (3:14–18)

Ant. The Lord is in our midst.

Shout for joy, daughter of Zion,
Israel, shout aloud!
Rejoice, exult with all your heart,
daughter of Jerusalem!
The Lord has repealed your sentence;
he has driven your enemies away.
The Lord, the king of Israel, is in your midst;
you have no more evil to fear.

When that day comes, word will come to
    Jerusalem:
Zion, have no fear,
do not let your hands fall limp.
The Lord your God is in your midst,
a victorious warrior.
He will exult with joy over you,
he will renew you by his love;
he will dance with shouts of joy for you
as on a day of festival.

Prayer

Come, Lord Jesus,
do not delay:
give new courage to your people
and by your coming
raise us to the joy of your kingdom.

The O Antiphons

Dec 17 O Wisdom,
      breath of the Most High,
      permeating all creation,
      you dispose all with strength and
          tenderness:
      O come and teach us the way of
          truth.

Dec 18 O Lord of lords
      and leader of the house of Israel,
      you appeared to Moses in the burning
          bush
      and gave him the Law on Sinai:
      O come and set us free.

Dec 19 O Flower of Jesse's stock,
      set up as a signal to the nations,
      kings stand mute before you
      and the nations do you homage:
      O come to deliver us,
      do not delay.

Dec 20 O Key of David
and ruler of the house of Israel;
who can open what you have closed
or close what you have opened?
O come and set your captive people
free.

Dec 21 O radiant Dawn,
splendor of eternal light
and sun of righteousness:
O come and shine on those who sit in
darkness
and in the shadow of death.

Dec 22 O King of all the nations,
the ruler they long for,
the cornerstone of the human family:
O come and save the creature you
fashioned from the dust.

Dec 23 O Emmanuel,
our ruler and our guide,
the awaited of the nations
and their Savior:
O come, Lord God, and set us free.

Marian Anthem for Advent

Mother of Christ, our hope, our patroness,
Star of the sea, our beacon in distress,
Guide to the shores of everlasting day
God's holy people on their pilgrim way.

Virgin, in you God made his dwelling place;
Mother of all the living, full of grace,
Blessed are you: God's word you did believe,
"Yes" on your lips undid the "No" of Eve.

Daughter of God, who bore his holy One,
Dearest of all to Christ, your loving Son,
Show us his face, O Mother, as on earth,
Loving us all, you gave our Savior birth.

Alma Redemptoris Mater
Trans. James Quinn, SJ

The Call

Come, my Way, my Truth, my Life:
Such a Way, as gives us breath:
Such a Truth, as ends all strife:
Such a Life, as killeth death.

Come, my Light, my Feast, my Strength:
Such a Light, as shows a feast:
Such a Feast, as mends in length:
Such a Strength, as makes his guest.

Come, my Joy, my Love, my Heart:
Such a Joy, as none can move:
Such a Love, as none can part:
Such a Heart, as joys in Love.

George Herbert (1593–1633)

Descend

Descend,
Holy Spirit of Life!
Come down into our hearts,
that we may live.
Descend into our emptiness,
that emptiness
may be filled.
Descend into the dust,
that the dust may flower.
Descend into the dark,
that the light
may shine in darkness.

Caryll Houselander (1901–1954)

Prayer

Christ our God,
fresh new Adam of our springing hope!
Uncontaminated by the world's
    estrangement,
leaping down from the bosom of Eternity,
issuing forth from the womb of new Eve, our
    Mother,
you are the inextinguishable light of a
    glowering universe.

Unstained by sin,
yet unshielded from sin's stratagems,

vulnerable yet unafraid—
O Divine Word of God—
dressed in our very flesh and blood,
endued with our mortality,
you are the yoke-fellow of humanity,
the pilgrim, the stranger, the exile
in this death-dark valley of tears.

God-Man,
clasp us by the heart
and lead us at long last
to the home-haven of heaven.

W. G. S.

Drop down dew, you heavens from above;
   you clouds, rain down the Just One.
      Let the earth open and bud forth a Savior.

Isaiah 45:8

Be a sign of his presence among all and
      bearers of joy.

Monks of Taizé

Christmastide

Hymn

A noble flow'r of Juda from tender roots has
    sprung,
A rose from stem of Jesse, as prophets long
    had sung,
A blossom fair and bright,
That in the midst of winter will change to
    dawn our night.

The rose of grace and beauty of which Isaiah
    sings
Is Mary, virgin mother, and Christ the flower
    she brings.
By God's divine decree
She bore our loving Savior, who died to set
    us free.

To Mary, dearest mother, with fervent hearts
    we pray:
Grant that your tender infant will cast our
    sins away,
And guide us with his love
That we shall ever serve him, and live with
    him above.

Psalm 19[a]   God's Glory Revealed in Christ

Ant. You are the Sun of righteousness, O
Christ our God.

How clearly the sky reveals God's glory!
How plainly it shows what he has done!
Each day announces it to the following day;
each night repeats it to the next.
No speech or words are used,
no sound is heard;
yet their voice goes out to all the world,
their message reaches the ends of the earth.

God set up a tent in the sky for the sun:
it comes out like a bridegroom striding from
     his house,
like an athlete, eager to run a race.
It starts at one end of the sky
and goes around to the other.
Nothing can hide from its heat.

Psalm Prayer

Father,
we are filled with the new light
by the coming of your Word among us.
May the light of faith
shine in our words and actions.
We ask this through Christ our Lord.
—Amen.

Canticle of the Word   John 1:1–5, 10–12, 14

Ant.   The Word was made flesh and dwelt
among us, alleluia.

In the beginning was the Word;
the Word was in God's presence,
and the Word was God.
He was present to God in the beginning.
Through him all things came into being,
and apart from him nothing came to be.
Whatever came to be in him found life,
life for the light of all.
The light shines on in darkness,
a darkness that did not overcome it.

He was in the world,
and through him the world was made,
yet the world did not know who he was.
To his own he came,
yet his own did not accept him.
Any who did accept him
he empowered to become children of God.

The Word became flesh
and made his dwelling among us,
and we have seen his glory:
the glory of an only Son coming from the
Father,
filled with enduring love. (NAB)

Prayer

Lord God,
we praise you for creating us,
and still more for restoring us in Christ.
Your Son shared our weakness:
may we share his glory.

Proclamation of the Nativity

Many ages after the creation of the world,
when God in the beginning made the
    heavens and the earth,
long after the Flood and the primeval
    covenant with Noah,
more than two thousand years after the
    promises
made to our father Abraham and to our
    mother Sarah,
fifteen centuries after Moses and Miriam and
    the Exodus from Egypt,
one thousand years after David was anointed
    king of Israel,
in the sixty-fifth week, according to the
    prophecy of Daniel,
in the one hundred and ninety-fourth
    Olympiad,
in the year seven-hundred and fifty-two from
    the founding of the city of Rome,
in the forty-second year of the emperor
    Octavian Augustus Caesar,

and in the sixth age of the world,
while the whole earth was at peace,
in order to consecrate the world by his
    gracious coming,
JESUS CHRIST,

eternal God and Son of the eternal Father,
conceived in time by the power of the Holy
    Spirit,
nine months having elapsed since his
    conception,
was born of the Virgin Mary in Bethlehem of
    Judah,
GOD MADE MAN.
THIS IS THE BIRTHDAY ACCORDING
TO THE FLESH
OF OUR LORD JESUS CHRIST.

The Roman Martyrology

The Nativity of Christ

This is the month, and this the happy morn,
Wherein the Son of Heaven's eternal King,
Of wedded Maid and Virgin Mother born,
Our great redemption from above did bring;
For so the holy sages once did sing,
  That he our deadly forfeit should release,
And with his Father work us a perpetual
    peace.

That glorious form, that light unsufferable,
And that far-beaming blaze of majesty,
Wherewith he wont at Heaven's high
    council-table
To sit the midst of Trinal Unity,
He laid aside; and here with us to be,
  Forsook the courts of everlasting day,
And chose with us a darksome house of
    mortal clay.

John Milton (1608–1674)

Prayer

Be born in us,
Incarnate Love.
Take our flesh and blood,
and give us your humanity;
take our lives, and give us your vision;
take our minds,
and give us your pure thought;
take our feet and set them in your path;
take our hands
and fold them in your prayer;
take our hearts
and give them your will to love.

Caryll Houselander (1901–1954)

New Things and Old

The dark is shattered
With wild, new fear;
An ass's feet stumbling
Is the sound that I hear.

The night is brighter
Than day should be;
A strange star's splendor
Is the light that I see.

And above the terror
Of earth and sky
I can hear, if I listen,
A young Child's cry;

I can see, if I look
Legions of wings,
And a woman who ponders
On all these things.

Sr. M. Madaleva, C.S.C. (1887–1964)

A Christmas Prayer

Lord God Almighty, Father of every family,
against whom no door can be shut:
Enter the homes of our land
with the angel of your presence,

to hallow them in pureness and beauty of
    love;
and by your dear Son, born in a stable,
move our hearts to hear the cry of the
    homeless,
and to convert all sordid and bitter dwellings
   into households of yours;
through Jesus Christ our Lord.
—Amen.

Lent

Hymn

Attend and keep this happy fast
I preach to you this day.
Is this the fast that pleases me
That takes your joy away?
Do I delight in sorrow's dress,
Says God who reigns above.
The hanging head, the dismal look—
Will they attract my love?

But is this not the fast I choose,
That shares the heavy load;
That seeks to bring the poor man in
Who's weary of the road;
That gives the hungry bread to eat,
To strangers gives a home;
That does not let you hide your face
From your own flesh and bone?

Then like the dawn your light will break;
To life you will be raised.
And they will praise the Lord for you;
Be happy in your days.
The glory of the Lord will shine,
And in your steps his grace.
And when you call he'll answer you;
He will not hide his face.

Based on Isaiah 58:5–9
Roger Ruston, 1970

Psalm 51 A Prayer for Forgiveness

Ant. If we die with the Lord, we shall live
with the Lord (1 Tim 2:13).

Have mercy on me, O God, in your
loving-kindness;
in your compassion blot out my offenses.
Wash me thoroughly from my iniquity,
and cleanse me from my sin.

I know full well my misdeeds,
and my sin is ever before me.
Against you, against you only, have I sinned,
and done what is evil in your sight.

You are just in your sentence,
and righteous in your judgment.
I was conceived in iniquity,
and I am a sinner from my mother's womb.

Yet you look for truth in my inmost being,
  and teach me wisdom in my heart.
Purify me that I may be clean;
  wash me, make me whiter than snow.

Let me hear joy and gladness,
  that the bones you have broken may
    rejoice.
Hide not your face from my sins,
  and wipe out all my iniquity.

Create in me a pure heart, O God,
  and renew a right spirit within me.
Cast me not away from your presence,
  and take not your holy Spirit from me.

Restore to me the joy of your salvation,
  and uphold me in a free will of obedience,
That I may teach transgressors your ways,
  and turn sinners back to you.

Deliver me from death, O God my savior,
  that my tongue may sing of your justice.
O Lord, open my lips,
  and my mouth shall proclaim your praise.

You have no delight in sacrifices;
  a burnt-offering from me would not please
    you.
The sacrifice you accept is a humble spirit;
  a broken and contrite heart, O God, you
    will not reject.

Psalm Prayer

Gracious Father,
when David repented before you in sackcloth
    and ashes,
you poured out on him
the healing medicine of your forgiveness.
Grant that we may follow his example so well
that we too may be fully pardoned of all our
    transgressions.
We make our prayer through Jesus our Lord.
—Amen.

Canticle of Zechariah (9:9–10) The Messianic
                       King

Ant. Hosanna to the Son of David!

Rejoice, rejoice, people of Zion!
    Shout for joy, you people of Jerusalem!
    Look, your king is coming to you!
He comes triumphant and victorious,
    but humble and riding on a donkey—
    on a colt, the foal of a donkey.

He will remove the war chariots from Israel
    and take the horses from Jerusalem;
    the bows used in battle will be destroyed.
Your king will make peace among the
    nations;
    he will rule from sea to sea,
from the river to the ends of the earth.

Prayer

Lord Jesus Christ,
you came among us first
as the suffering Servant of God.
When you come again in glory
to judge the living and the dead,
be our peace and our salvation,
for you have redeemed us with your precious
    blood.
You live and reign for ever and ever.
—Amen.

Happiness and Sorrow   (Lk 6:20–26)

Happy are you poor;
    the Kingdom of God is yours!
Happy are you who are hungry now;
    you will be filled!
Happy are you who weep now;
    you will laugh!
Happy are you when people hate you,
    reject you, insult you,
    and say that you are evil,
    all because of the Son of Man!
    Be glad when that happens and dance for
        joy,
    because a great reward is kept for you in
        heaven.
    For their ancestors did the very same
        things to the prophets.

205

But how terrible for you who are rich now;
    you have had your easy life!
How terrible for you who are full now;
    you will go hungry!
How terrible for you who laugh now;
    you will mourn and weep!
How terrible when all people speak well of
    you;
    their ancestors said the very same things
    about the false prophets.

Hear, O Lord

Ant. Hear us, O Lord, and have mercy,
       for we have sinned in your sight
       (Bar 3:2).

King high exalted,
all the world's Redeemer,
to you your children
lift their eyes with weeping;
Christ, we implore you,
hear our supplications.

Right hand of Godhead,
headstone of the corner,
path of salvation,
gate to heaven's kingdom,
cleanse your sinful people
stained with transgressions.

On our knees before you,
majesty eternal,
we lament our sinfulness
in your holy hearing.

Humbly now confessing,
countless sins admitting,
we lay bare our secrets;
may your boundless mercy
grant to us full pardon.

Captive led away,
guiltless, unresisting,
charged by false witness,
unto death for sinners,
Jesus Christ protect us
whom your blood has purchased.

Attende Domine

Consider Well

Consider well that both by night and day
  While we most busily provide and care
For our disport, our revel, and our play,
  For pleasant melody and dainty fare,
  Death stealeth on full slily; unaware
He lieth at hand and shall us all surprise,
We wot not when nor where nor in what
    wise.

When fierce temptations threat thy soul with
    loss
  Think on his passion and the bitter pain,
Think on the mortal anguish of the cross,
    Think on Christ's blood let out at every
    vein,
    Think on his precious heart all rent in
    twain;
For thy redemption think all this was
    wrought,
Nor be that lost which he so dearly bought.

St. Thomas More (1478–1535)

Christ Crucified

Thy restless feet cannot go
  For us and our eternal good,
As they were ever wont. What though
  They swim, alas! in their own flood?

Thy hands to give thou canst not lift,
  Yet will thy hand still giving be;
It gives, but O, itself's the gift!
  It gives though bound; though bound 'tis
  free!

Richard Crashaw (1612–1649)

Wardrobe

My love gave me a king's robe,
Mock purple and red;
My love gave me a white coat,
A fool's coat, he said;
My love gave me a weft crown
Of thorns for my head.
Because he is my true love
He wore them instead.

Sr. M. Madaleva, CSC (1887–1964)

King of Friday

O King of Friday
Whose limbs were stretched on the cross,
O Lord who did suffer
The bruises, the wounds, the loss,
We stretch ourselves
Beneath the shield of thy might,
Some fruit from the tree of thy passion
Fall on us this night!

From the Irish

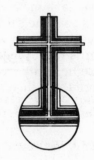

Holy Week

**In Honor of The Five Wounds
of Our Lord Jesus Christ**

In honor of the wound in the right hand:

Praise and glory to you, Lord Jesus,
for the holy wound in your right hand.
Through this wound of love,
forgive all the sins I have committed
in thought, word and deed,
by neglect of your service,
and by my self-indulgence,
both waking and sleeping.
Help me to keep your death on the cross
and your sacred wounds always before my
    mind
and may my gratitude express itself
by the daily shouldering of my own cross.
Grant this, Lord Jesus,
you who live and reign for ever and ever.
Amen.

The Year of Our Lord

In honor of the wound in the left hand:

Praise and glory to you, Lord Jesus,
for the wound in your left hand.
Through this wound of love,
have mercy on me and remove from my heart
   all that displeases you.
Grant me victory over the relentless enemies
   who wage war against me.
Fill me with your strength so that I may
   trample upon them all.
Through your merciful death
deliver me from all the dangers
to which my life and my salvation are
   exposed
and make me worthy of sharing in your
   glorious kingdom.
You live and reign for ever and ever.
Amen.

In honor of the wound in the right foot:

Praise and glory to you, O Jesus, good
   Savior,
for the holy wound in your right foot.
Through this wound of love,
grant that I may truly repent
in proportion to the magnitude of my sins.
Through your death on the cross
keep this community of ours
continually united to your will

and preserve it body and spirit from all
    adversity.
When the dreadful day of judgment comes,
receive my soul into your mercy
and grant it eternal joy, O Lord,
you who live and reign for ever and ever.
Amen.

In honor of the wound in the left foot:

Praise and glory to you, merciful Jesus,
for the holy wound in your left foot.
Through this wound of love,
grant me full pardon of all my sins,
so that by your help, before dying,
I may receive the sacrament of your body and
    blood,
confess all my sins with perfect contrition,
be anointed for glory
and pass on to you in complete purity of
    body and mind.
Hear my prayer, O Lord,
you who live and reign for ever and ever.
Amen.

In honor of the wound in the side:

Praise and glory to you, O Jesus, worthy of
    all our love,
for the holy wound in your side.
Through this wound of love,

we see your immense mercy revealed,
not only to the soldier who pierced your
   heart,
but to us all.
Reborn in baptism,
I am now being delivered from every evil,
past, present and yet to come,
through the merits of your precious blood
offered and received in all the world.
By your bitter death,
grant me lively faith, unshakable hope and
   perfect charity,
so that I may love you with all my heart and
   mind and strength.
Establish me in your holy ways,
so that I may courageously persevere in your
   service
and please you now and always.
Amen.

We adore you O Christ, and we praise you,
—for by your holy cross you have redeemed
   the world.

      Let us pray.

Almighty and eternal God,
you redeemed the human race through the
   five wounds of your Son,
our Lord Jesus Christ.

As we worship these wounds of love day by
    day,
rescue us from a sudden and eternal death
by the merits of his blood and his own dying.
We ask this through the same Lord Jesus,
who lives and reigns with you and the Holy
    Spirit,
one God, for ever and ever.
Amen.

              St. Clare of Assisi (1194–1253)
                    Trans. W.G.S.

Easter

Hymn

Who is this who comes to us in triumph,
Clothed in royal garments dyed with blood,
Walking in the greatness of his glory,
Bearing in his hand the holy rood?

This is Christ the risen Lord, the Strong One,
He who trod the winepress all alone;
Out of death he comes with life unending,
Seeking those he purchased for his own.

Great and wonderful is our Redeemer,
Christ the Living One, the just and true,
Praise him with the Father and the Spirit,
Ever with us, making all things new.

Based on Isaiah 63:1–7
Stanbrook Abbey Hymnal

Psalm 118   Christ Declares the Rescuing
Power of God

Ant. Alleluia, alleluia, alleluia!

Give thanks to the Lord for he is good;
  his loving-kindness endures for ever.
The right hand of the Lord has triumphed!
The right hand of the Lord is exalted!
The right hand of the Lord is victorious!

I shall not die but live,
  to declare the deeds of the Lord.
He has given me a sore punishment,
  but he has not handed me over to death.

Open to me the gates of victory,
  that I may enter and give thanks to the
    Lord.

  "This is the gate of the Lord;
  the righteous may enter it."
I thank you because you answered me;
  and you have become my salvation.

  "The stone that the builders rejected
  has become the chief cornerstone."

This is the Lord's doing;
  it is marvelous in our sight.

"This is the day when the Lord has
acted;
let us rejoice and be glad in it!"

Hosanna! Hosanna!
Save us, Lord, and prosper us, we pray.

"Blessed is he who comes in the Name of
the Lord;
we bless you from the house of the
Lord."

Give thanks to the Lord for he is good;
his loving-kindness endures for ever.

Psalm Prayer

Lord Jesus Christ,
by your cross and resurrection,
you have destroyed death
and brought life to those in the grave.
May your blessed passion be the joy of the
whole world
and may the glory of your rising from the
tomb
ever be our song,
O Savior of the world,
living and reigning with the Father and the
Holy Spirit,
now and for ever.
—Amen.

Marian Anthem for Eastertide

Joy fill your heart, O Queen most high,
    alleluia!
Your son who in the tomb did lie, alleluia!
Has risen as he did prophesy, alleluia!
Pray for us, Mother, when we die, alleluia!

Regina Coeli
Trans. James Quinn, S.J.

Easter Sequence

O flock of Christ, your homage bring
To Christ the Lamb, your glorious King!
His Easter praise in triumph sing!
Alleluia, alleluia, alleluia!

Peace has come down from God on high!
The King of peace in death did lie!
To save the sheep the Lamb did die!

Never on earth was stranger sight:
Life fought with death in darkest night,
Yet lives to reign in endless light!

What saw you, Mary, on your way?
"I saw the tomb where Life once lay,
Whose glory shone this Easter Day!

Angels their joyful tidings spread!
Grave-clothes I saw where none lay dead,
The cloth that once had veiled his head!

Christ is my hope, who rose for me!
Soon will you all his glory see!
Christ bids you go to Galilee!"

Christ has indeed aris'n again
As Lord of life, to rule all men!
On us have mercy, Lord! Amen.
Alleluia, alleluia, alleluia!

> *Victimae Paschali Laudes*
> *Trans. James Quinn, S.J.*

Easter Anthem—Christ Our Passover
(1 Cor 5:7–8; Rom 6:9–11; 1 Cor 15:20–22)

Alleluia.
Christ our Passover has been sacrificed for
     us;
   therefore let is keep the feast,
Not with the old leaven, the leaven of malice
     and evil,
   but with the unleavened bread of sincerity
     and truth. Alleluia.

Christ being raised from the dead will never
     die again;
   death no longer has dominion over him.
The death that he died, he died to sin, once
     for all;
   but the life he lives, he lives to God.

So also consider yourselves dead to sin,
  and alive to God in Jesus Christ our Lord.
    Alleluia.

Christ has been raised from the dead,
  the first fruits of those who have fallen
    asleep.
For since by a man came death,
  by a man has come also the resurrection of
    the dead.
For as in Adam all die,
  so also in Christ shall all be made alive.
    Alleluia.

Book of Common Prayer

Prayer

Almighty and ever-living God,
you sealed a covenant of reconciliation with
    us
in the mystery of Christ's passing from death
    to life.
May we come to everlasting joy
by a holy keeping of these Easter festivities.
We ask this through Christ our risen Lord.
—Amen.

The Victorious Cross

We adore you, Lord Jesus Christ, as you
     ascend your cross.
May this cross deliver us from the destroying
     angel.

We adore your wounded body as it hangs on
     the cross.
May your wounds be our healing.

We adore you dead and buried in the tomb.
May your death be our life.

We adore you as you descend among the
     dead to deliver them.
May we never hear the dread sentence of
     doom.

We adore you rising from the dead.
Free us from the weight of our sins.

We adore you ascending to the right hand of
     God your Father.
Raise us to eternal glory along with all your
     saints.

We adore you as you come to judge the living
     and the dead.
At your coming be not our Judge but our
     Savior.

Holy Cross,
>You are more exalted than all the trees of
>   the forest:
>on you hung the life of the world;
>on you Christ proceeded to his triumph;
>on you death overcame death.

Holy God, Holy Mighty One, Holy Immortal
>One:
who take away the sins of the world,
have mercy on us

>*From a 10th-century manuscript*
>*Trans. W.G.S.*

The Cosmic Christ

I see his blood upon the rose
And in the stars the glory of his eyes,
His body gleams amid eternal snows,
His tears fall from the skies.

I see his face in every flower;
The thunder and the singing of the birds
Are but his voice—and carven by his power,
Rocks are his written words.

All pathways by his feet are worn,
His strong heart stirs the ever-beating sea,
His crown of thorns is twined with every
>   thorn,
His cross is every tree.

>*Joseph M. Plunkett (1887–1916)*
224

Christ in the Universe

With this ambiguous earth
His dealings have been told us. These abide:
The signal to a maid, the humble birth,
The lesson, and the young Man crucified.

But not a star of all
The innumerable host of stars has heard
How he administered this terrestrial ball.
Our race have kept their Lord's entrusted
    Word.

Of his earth-visiting feet
None knows the secret, cherished, perilous,
The terrible, shamefast, frightened,
    whispered, sweet,
Heart-shattering secret of his way with us.

No planet knows that this
Our wayside planet, carrying land and wave,
Love and life multiplied, and pain and bliss,
Bears, as chief treasure, one forsaken grave.

Alice Meynell (1847–1922)

Easter Day

Earth breaks up, time drops away,
In flows Heaven, with its new day
Of endless life, when he who trod,
Very Man and very God,

This earth in weakness, shame and pain,
Dying the death whose signs remain
Up yonder on the accursed tree,—
Shall come again, no more to be
Of captivity the thrall,
But the one God, all in all,
King of Kings, Lord of Lords.

Robert Browning (1812–1889)

An Easter Prayer

"He is risen"
That through him we may rediscover faith:
in ourselves
in our world
in our God.
"He is risen"
That in him we may rekindle hope:
for the abandoned
for the despairing
for the dreamless.
"He is risen"
That with him we may restore love:
to those from whom we have kept it
to those who are most near us
to those we will never meet—
to all and everything.
"He is risen"
Amen.

Christopher Prayers for Today

Thanksgiving for Baptism

We give you heartfelt thanks, most merciful
    Father,
for receiving us through Baptism as your own
    dear children
and for incorporating us into your holy
    Church:
and we humbly ask that,
as we are partakers of the death of your Son,
so we may also be partakers of his
    resurrection,
and may finally, with your whole Church,
be inheritors of your everlasting kingdom;
through the same Jesus Christ our Lord.

We are an Easter people
and ALLELUIA is our song.

St. Augustine (354–430)

Pentecost and the Church

Sequence of Pentecost

Holy Spirit, font of light,
    focus of God's glory bright,
    shed on us a shining ray.
Father of the fatherless,
    giver of gifts limitless,
    come and touch our hearts today.

Source of strength and sure relief,
    comforter in time of grief,
    enter in and be our guest.
On our journey grant us aid,
    freshening breeze and cooling shade,
    in our labor inward rest.

Enter each aspiring heart,
    occupy its inmost part
    with your dazzling purity.
All that gives to human worth,
    all that benefits the earth,
    you bring to maturity.

With your soft refreshing rains
    break our drought, remove our stains;
    bind up all our injuries.
Shake with rushing wind our will;
    melt with fire our icy chill;
    bring to light our perjuries.

As your promise we believe
    make us ready to receive
    gifts from your unbounded store.
Grant enabling energy,
    courage in adversity,
    joys that last for evermore.

Veni, Sancte Spiritus
Trans. John Webster Grant

Prophecy of the Spirit

This is what I will do in the
    last days, God says:
I will pour out my Spirit on
    everyone.
Your sons and daughters will
    proclaim my message;
Your young men will see
    visions,
and your old men will have
    dreams.
Yes, even on my servants,
    both men and women,

230

I will pour out my Spirit in
   those days,
and they will proclaim my
   message.
I will perform miracles in the
   sky above
and wonders on the earth
   below.

Acts 2:17–19 (cf. Joel 2:28–32)

Prayer

Come down upon us,
Spirit of God,
spirit of wisdom
and peace and joy;
come as a great wind blowing;
sweep our minds with a storm of light.
Be in us as bright fire burning;
forge our wills to shining swords
in the flame.
Purify our hearts
in the crucible
of the fire of love.
Change our tepid nature
into the warm humanity
of Christ,
as he changed water into wine.
Be in us a stream of life,
as wine in the living vine.

Caryll Houselander (1901–1954)

231

Pentecost

Jubilation is my name and rejoicing is my
 countenance,
  I am like a young meadow wreathed in
   dawn,
Like a sweet shepherd's pipe among the hills.
Hear me ye swelling valleys; hear me, ye
  waving meadows;
  hear me, ye happy songful forests.
For I am no longer lonely among your
  splendors;
  I have become your sister and one of your
   kin:
  greet me, fair likeness of myself,
  glad earth that the Lord has fulfilled.
Nearness is still far; grace is yet but an
  upward step;
  He is in me as eternally mine.
He has come over me as buds come on a
  spray,
  he has sprung forth in me like roses on the
   hedgerows.
I bloom in the red-thorn of his love,
  I bloom on all my branches in the purple of
   his gifts.
I bloom with fiery tongues,
  I bloom with flaming fulfilment,
  I bloom out of the Holy Spirit of God.

Gertrud von Le Fort (1876–1971)

Promise of the Spirit

I will ask the Father,
and he will give you another Helper,
who will stay with you forever.
He is the Spirit,
who reveals the truth about God.
The world cannot receive him,
because it cannot see him or know him.
But you know him,
because he remains with you and is in you.

I have told you this
while I am still with you.
The Helper, the Holy Spirit,
whom the Father will send in my name,
will teach you everything
and make you remember all that I have told
     you.

I am telling you the truth:
it is better for you that I go away,
because if I do not go,
the Helper will not come to you.
But if I do go away,
Then I will send him to you.

When the Spirit comes,
who reveals the truth about God,
he will lead you into all the truth.

Jn 14:16–17, 25–26; 16:7, 13.

Prayer

Lord, give us your Spirit.
Grant us the fruits of the Spirit:
love, joy, peace, patience, kindness, goodness,
faithfulness, humility and self-control (Gal 5:22).
If we have the Spirit and his fruits,
then we are no longer slaves of the law
but free children of God.
The Spirit cries out in us: Abba, Father.
He intercedes for us with unspeakable
      groanings.
He is the anointing, the seal and surety of
      eternal life.
He is the fount of eternal water
which has its source in the heart
and rises up to eternal life, whispering:
Come! Come home to the Father!

Jesus, send us the Spirit.
Give us again and again your pentecostal
      gift.
Make our spiritual eye bright
and our spiritual awareness sensitive,
so that we are able to distinguish your Spirit
      from all others.
Give us your Spirit, that it may be said of us:
If the Spirit of God, who raised Jesus from death,
lives in you,
then he who raised Christ from death

will also give life to your mortal bodies
by the presence of his Spirit in you (Rom 8:11).

Lord, may Pentecost be ever with us.
Your servants and handmaids ask with the
    boldness you require of them:
May Pentecost be in us also.
Now and for ever. Amen.

Karl Rahner

God's Grandeur

The world is charged with the grandeur of
    God.
  It will flame out, like shining from shook
    foil;
  It gathers to a greatness, like the ooze of oil
Crushed. Why do men then now not reck his
    rod?
Generations have trod, have trod, have trod;
  And all is seared with trade; bleared,
    smeared with toil;
  And wears man's smudge and shares
    man's smell: the soil
Is bare now, nor can foot feel, being shod.

And for all this, nature is never spent;
  There lives the dearest freshness deep
    down things;
And though the last lights off the black West
    went

235

Oh, morning, at the brown brink eastward,
  springs—
Because the Holy Ghost over the bent
  World broods with warm breast and with
  ah! bright wings.

Gerard Manley Hopkins (1844–1889)

Coming of the Spirit

Jesus gave them this order:
"Do not leave Jerusalem,
but wait for the gift
I told you about,
the gift my Father promised.
John baptized with water,
but in a few days you will be
baptized with the Holy Spirit.

"When the Holy Spirit comes upon you
you will be filled with power,
and you will be witnesses for me
in Jerusalem,
in all of Judea and Samaria,
and to the ends of the earth."

When the day of Pentecost came,
all the believers were gathered together
in one place.
Suddenly there was a noise from the sky
which sounded like a strong wind blowing,

and it filled the whole house
where they were sitting.
Then they saw what looked like
tongues of fire
which spread out and touched
each person there.
They were all filled with
the Holy Spirit.

Acts 1:4–5, 8; 2:1–4

Morning Prayer to the Holy Spirit

O Holy and astounding Spirit,
You catch me by surprise at least once a day
    with the freshness of your love
    and the unpredictability of your
    presence—
    especially in humble things
    that somehow give me immense joy.
Some moments are completely new, full of
    joy,
    as uplifting as the dawning sun,
    and those moments come from you,
      day by day.
Stand behind me today when I'm right and
    ought to be more determined,
    and block my way when I'm being
      stupid and ought to back off.
Teach me true compassion for those in need,
    so I can be of genuine help to someone.
Bless me, today, Holy Spirit, and astound me
    again!

Tom Noe

To the Holy Spirit

O Holy Spirit, Paraclete,
perfect in us the work begun by Jesus;
enable us to continue to pray fervently
in the name of the whole world.

Hasten in every one of us the growth of a
     deep interior life;
give vigor to our apostolate
so that it may reach all peoples,
all redeemed by the blood of Christ and all
     belonging to him. . . .
Let no earthly bond prevent us from
     honoring our vocation,
no cowardly considerations disturb the claims
     of justice,
no meanness confine the immensity of
     charity
within the narrow bounds of petty
     selfishness.
Let everything in us be on a grand scale:
the search for truth, and the devotion to it,
and readiness for self-sacrifice, even to the
     cross and death;
and may everything finally
be according to your will,
O Holy Spirit of love,
which the Father and the Son desired
to be poured out over the Church and its
     institutions,
over each and every human soul and over
     nations.

Pope John XXIII (1881–1963)

Your Spirit, Lord, Is Truth

Come to us, Spirit of the Lord!

Your Spirit, Lord, is truth:
May it make us free.
Come to us, Spirit of the Lord!

Your Spirit, Lord, is fire:
May it enkindle us with love.
Come to us, Spirit of the Lord!

Your Spirit, Lord, is gentleness:
may it bring us peace.
Come to us, Spirit of the Lord!

Your Spirit, Lord, renews the face of the
    earth:
may it renew the depths of our hearts.
Come to us, Spirit of the Lord!

Your Spirit, Lord, is prayer:
may it open our hearts to give praise.
Come to us, Spirit of the Lord!

Your Spirit, Lord, fills the whole universe:
may it live among us forever.
Come to us, Spirit of the Lord!

Your Spirit, Lord, is life:
may it raise us up on the last day.
Come to us, Spirit of the Lord!

Lucien Deiss

The Church's Greatest Need

What does the Church need?
The Church needs the Spirit,
the Holy Spirit.
He it is who animates and sanctifies the
    Church.
He is her divine breath,
the wind in her sails,
the principle of her unity,
the inner source of her light and strength.
He is her support and consoler,
her source of charisms and songs,
her peace and her joy,
her pledge and prelude to blessed and eternal
    life.

The Church needs her perennial Pentecost.
She needs fire in her heart,
words on her lips,
prophecy in her outlook.
She needs to be the temple of the Holy Spirit.

In the empty silence of the modern world
the Church needs to feel rising
from the depths of her inmost personality,
a weeping, a poem, a prayer, a hymn—
the praying voice of the Spirit,
who prays in us and for us
"with sighs too deep for words."

She needs to listen in silence
and in an attitude of total availability
to the voice of the Spirit
who teaches "every truth."

The Church needs to feel flowing
through all her human faculties
a wave of love,
that love which is called forth
and poured into our hearts
"by the Holy Spirit who has been given to
    us."

This is what the Church needs;
she needs the Holy Spirit!
The Holy Spirit in us,
in each of us,
and in all of us together,
in us who are the Church.

So let all of us ever say to him,
"Come."

Pope Paul VI (1897–1978)

O divine Spirit . . . renew in our own days
    your miracles as of a second Pentecost.

Pope John XXIII (1881–1963)

5. Night Prayer

As EACH DAY draws to a close, we commend ourselves into the hands of our heavenly Father. God freely forgives us our daily faults, refreshes us with sleep, and conducts us safely through the night to another day of love and service.

When this office is prayed with others, the stanzas of the psalms, the hymn and the Song of Simeon may be alternated between the leader and the group *or* the group may divide in two and alternate the stanzas in that fashion. The antiphons are recited by all before and after the psalm and the Song of Simeon.

I. Confession

Leader: Our help + is in the name of the Lord,

All: The maker of heaven and earth.

Leader: Let us confess our sins to God and to one another.

(*Brief examination of conscience*)

All: I confess to Almighty God
and to you, my brothers and sisters,
that I have sinned through my own
     fault
in my thoughts and in my words,
in what I have done,
and in what I have failed to do;
and I ask blessed Mary, ever virgin,
all the angels and saints,
and you, my brothers and sisters,
to pray for me to the Lord our God.

Leader: May almighty God have mercy on us, forgive us our sins,
and bring us to everlasting life.

All: Amen.

II. Psalmody

(Pray the appropriate psalm and psalm prayer for the day and then turn to page 259 for the concluding parts of night prayer.)

Sunday   Psalm 91—God's Sheltering Care

Ant. I have given you the power to tread
upon serpents and scorpions.

(Lk 10:19)

Whoever goes to the Most High for safety,
   whoever remains under the protection of
      the Almighty,
can say to him, "You are my defender and
      protector.
   You are my God; in you I trust."

He will keep you safe from all hidden
      dangers
   and from all deadly diseases.
He will cover you with his wings;
   you will be safe in his care;
   his faithfulness will protect and defend
      you.
You need not fear any dangers at night
   or sudden attacks during the day
   or the plagues that strike in the dark
   or the evils that kill in daylight.

A thousand may fall dead beside you,
ten thousand all around you,
but you will not be harmed.
You will look and see
how the wicked are punished.

You have made the Lord your defender,
the Most High your protector,
and so no disaster will strike you,
no violence will come near your home.
God will put his angels in charge of you
to protect you wherever you go.
They will hold you up with their hands
to keep you from hurting your feet on the
stones.
You will trample down lions and snakes,
fierce lions and poisonous snakes.

God says, "I will save those who love me
and will protect those who know me as
Lord.
When they call to me, I will answer them;
when they are in trouble, I will be with
them.
I will rescue them and honor them.
I will reward them with long life;
I will save them."

Glory to the Father, and to the Son, and to
the Holy Spirit:
as it was in the beginning, is now, and will
be for ever.   Amen.

Ant. I have given you the power to tread
upon serpents and scorpions.

Psalm Prayer

Leader: Let us pray (*Pause for silent prayer*).

Lord Jesus Christ,
when tempted by the devil,
you remained loyal to your Father
whose angels watched over you at
his command.
Guard your Church and keep us
from the plague of sin
so that we may remain loyal
to the day we enjoy your salvation
and glory.
You live and reign for ever and ever.

All: Amen.

Monday Psalm 4—We Trust in God's Care

Ant. Be kind to me now, O Lord, and hear
my prayer.

Answer me when I pray,
·O God, my defender!
When I was in trouble, you helped me.
Be kind to me now and hear my prayer.

How long will you people insult me?
How long will you love what is worthless
and go after what is false?

Remember that the Lord has chosen the
righteous for his own,
and he hears me when I call to him.

Tremble with fear and stop sinning;
think deeply about this,
when you lie in silence on your beds.
Offer the right sacrifices to the Lord,
and put your trust in him.

There are many who pray:
"Give us more blessings, O Lord.
. Look on us with kindness!"
But the joy that you have given me
is more than they will ever have
with all their grain and wine.

When I lie down, I go to sleep in peace;
you alone, O Lord, keep me perfectly safe.

Glory to the Father, and to the Son, and to
the Holy Spirit:
as it was in the beginning, is now, and will
be for ever.   Amen.

Ant. Be kind to me now, O Lord, and hear
my prayer.

Psalm Prayer

Leader: Let us pray (*Pause for silent prayer*).

You consoled your Son in his
anguish
and released him from the darkness
of the grave.
Lord, turn your face toward us
that we may sleep in your peace
and rise in your light.
We ask this through Christ our Lord.

All: Amen.

Tuesday Psalm 16—A Prayer of Confidence

Ant. The Father raised up Jesus from the
dead and broke the bonds of death
(Acts 2:24).

Protect me, O God; I trust in you for safety.
I say to the Lord, "You are my Lord;
all the good things I have come from you."

How excellent are the Lord's faithful people!
My greatest pleasure is to be with them.

You, Lord are all I have,
  and you give me all I need;
  my future is in your hands.
How wonderful are your gifts to me;
  how good they are!
I am always aware of the Lord's presence;
  he is near, and nothing can shake me.

And so I am thankful and glad,
  and I feel completely secure,
because you protect me from the power of
    death,
  and the one you love you will not abandon
  to the world of the dead.

You will show me the path that leads to life;
  your presence fills me with joy
  and brings me pleasure for ever.

Glory to the Father, and to the Son, and to
    the Holy Spirit:
  as it was in the beginning, is now, and will
  be for ever.   Amen.

Ant. The Father raised up Jesus from the
          dead and broke the bonds of death.

Psalm Prayer

Leader: Let us pray (*Pause for silent prayer*).

          Lord Jesus,
          uphold those who hope in you

and give us your counsel,
so that we may know the joy of your
resurrection
and deserve to be among the saints
at your right hand.
You live and reign for ever and ever.

All: Amen.

Wednesday Psalm 31:1–5—Trustful Prayer
in Adversity

Ant. Father, into your hands I commend my
spirit (Lk 23:46).

I come to you, Lord, for protection;
never let me be defeated.
You are a righteous God; save me, I pray!
Hear me! Save me now!
Be my refuge to protect me;
my defense to save me.

You are my refuge and defense;
guide me and lead me as you have
promised.
Keep me safe from the trap that has been set
for me;
shelter me from danger.
I place myself in your care.
You will save me, Lord;
you are a faithful God.

252

Glory to the Father, and to the Son, and to
   the Holy Spirit:
  as it was in the beginning, is now, and will
  be for ever.   Amen.

Ant. Father, into your hands I commend my
         spirit.

Psalm Prayer

Leader: Let us pray (*Pause for silent prayer*).

          Full of trust we run to you, Lord,
          and put our lives into your hands.
          You are our strength in times of
               trouble
          and our refuge along the way.
          May you be our joy at the turning
               points of life
          and our reward at its end.
          We make our prayer through Jesus
               the Lord.

All: Amen.

Thursday   Psalm 139:1–12—God Sees and
Cares for All

Ant. Darkness and light are the same to you,
O Lord.

Lord, you have examined me and you know
me.
You know everything I do;
from far away you understand all my
thoughts.
You see me, whether I am working or
resting;
you know all my actions.

Even before I speak,
you already know what I will say.
You are all around me on every side;
you protect me with your power.
Your knowledge of me is too deep;
it is beyond my understanding.

Where could I go to escape from you?
Where could I get away from your
presence?
If I went up to heaven, you would be there.
If I lay down in the world of the dead, you
would be there.
If I flew away beyond the east,
or lived in the farthest place in the west,
you would be there to lead me,
you would be there to help me.

I could ask the darkness to hide me,
   or the light around me to turn into night,
but even darkness is not dark for you,
   and the night is as bright as the day.
   Darkness and light are the same to you.

Glory to the Father, and to the Son, and to
      the Holy Spirit:
   as it was in the beginning, is now, and will
      be for ever.   Amen.

Ant. Darkness and light are the same to you,
         O Lord.

Psalm Prayer

Leader: Let us pray (*Pause for silent prayer*).

         You watch over heaven and earth,
            Lord Jesus.
         Your death brought light to the
            dead;
         your resurrection gave joy to the
            saints;
         your ascension made the angels
            rejoice.
         Lead us to eternal life,
         and watch over us with your love.
         You live and reign for ever and ever.

All: Amen.

Friday Psalm 130—A Cry for Help

Ant. He will save his people from their sins
(Mt 1:21).

From the depths of my despair I call to you,
Lord.
  Hear my cry, O Lord;
  Listen to my call for help.
If you kept a record of our sins,
  who could escape being condemned?
But you forgive us,
  so that we should reverently obey you.

I wait eagerly for the Lord's help,
  and in his word I trust.
I wait for the Lord
  more eagerly than watchmen wait for the
  dawn—
  than watchmen wait for the dawn.

Israel, trust in the Lord,
  because his love is constant
  and he is always willing to save.
He will save his people Israel
  from all their sins.

Glory to the Father, and to the Son, and to
  the Holy Spirit:
  as it was in the beginning, is now, and will
  be for ever.   Amen.

Ant. He will save his people from their sins.

Psalm Prayer

Leader: Let us pray (*Pause for silent prayer*).

God of might and compassion,
you sent your Word into the world,
a watchman to announce the dawn
 of salvation.
Do not leave us in the depths of our
 sins
but listen to your Church pleading
 with you.
Respond to her trust,
and pour out in her the fullness of
 your redeeming grace.
Please grant this through Christ our
 Lord.

All: Amen.

Saturday Psalm 134—We Praise God
        through the Night

Ant. Praise God, all you his servants, small
   and great (Rev. 19:5).

Come, praise the Lord, all you his servants,
 all who serve in his Temple at night.
Raise your hands in prayer in the Temple,
 and praise the Lord!

May the Lord, who made heaven and earth,
  bless you from Zion!

Glory to the Father, and to the Son, and to
  the Holy Spirit:
    as it was in the beginning, is now, and will
    be for ever.   Amen.

Ant. Praise God, all you his servants, small
            and great.

Psalm Prayer

Leader: Let us pray (*Pause for silent prayer*).

            All your servants praise and thank
                you, Lord.
            Be our light as night descends.
            We lift up to you the good works of
                our hands;
            grant us your generous blessing.
            We ask this through Christ our Lord.

All: Amen.

III. Hymn

O radiant Light, O Sun divine
Of God the Father's deathless face,
O image of the light sublime
That fills the heavenly dwelling place:

O Son of God, the source of life,
Praise is your due by night and day;
Our happy lips must raise the strain
Of your esteemed and splendid name.

Lord Jesus Christ, as daylight fades,
As shine the lights of eventide,
We praise the Father with the Son,
The Spirit blest and with them one.

Phos Hilaron

IV. Reading

(One of the following scripture passages is read.)

Remember this! The Lord—and the Lord
alone—is our God. Love the Lord your God
with all your heart, with all your soul, and
with all your strength. Never forget these
commands that I am giving you today. Teach
them to your children. Repeat them when you
are at home and when you are away, when
you are resting and when you are working.

Dt 6:4–7

All: Thanks be to God.

Be alert, be on the watch! Your enemy, the Devil, roams around like a roaring lion, looking for someone to devour. Be firm in your faith and resist him.   *I Peter 5:8–9*

All: Thanks be to God.

Surely, Lord, you are with us! We are your people; do not abandon us.   *Jeremiah 14:9*

All: Thanks be to God.

Responsory

Leader: Into your hands, O Lord, I
            commend my spirit.

All: Into your hands, O Lord, I
            commend my spirit.

Leader: You have redeemed us, Lord God of
            Truth.

All: I commend my spirit.

Leader: Glory to the Father, and to the Son,
            and to the Holy Spirit.

All: Into your hands, O Lord, I
            commend my spirit.

V. Song of Simeon

Ant. Guard us, O Lord, while we are awake
and keep us while we sleep,
that waking we may watch with Christ
and sleeping we may rest in peace.

Luke 2:29–32

Lord, + now let your servant go in peace;
your word has been fulfilled:
my own eyes have seen the salvation
which you have prepared in the sight of
every people:
a light to reveal you to the nations
and the glory of your people Israel.

Glory to the Father, and to the Son, and to the
Holy Spirit:
as it was in the beginning, is now, and will be
for ever. Amen.

Ant. Guard us, O Lord, while we are awake
and keep us while we sleep,
that waking we may watch with Christ
and sleeping we may rest in peace.

VI. Prayer

(The leader then says one of the following prayers.)

Lighten our darkness, O Lord,
and by your great mercy
defend us from all perils and
    dangers
of this coming night;
for the love of your only Son, our
    Savior Jesus Christ.

All: Amen.

Lord Jesus Christ, Son of the living
    God,
at the evening hour you rested in the
    sepulchre,
and sanctified the grave to be a bed
    of hope for your people.
Make us so repentant for our sins,
which were the cause of your
    Passion,
that when our bodies lie in the dust,
our souls may live with you
for ever and ever.

All: Amen.

Lord,
fill this night with your radiance.
May we sleep in peace and rise with
    joy
to welcome the light of a new day in
    your name.
We ask this through Christ our Lord.

All: Amen.

VII. Conclusion

Leader: May all who have died in Christ rest
    in his peace.

All: Amen.

Leader: May the Lord give + us a peaceful
    night as day's perfect ending.

All: Amen.

There is only one sadness: not to be a saint.
                              Georges Bernanos

6. Litanies

OUR LORD NOT ONLY taught us to pray but he commanded us to pray: insistently, perseveringly, without ceasing (Mt 7:7–11; Mk 11:20–25; Lk 11:1–22; 18:1–8). In Christian devotion, one of the ways of persisting in prayer is through the use of litanies which invoke God, Christ, the Blessed Virgin, St. Joseph and other saints under a variety of titles and ascriptions of honor. Only the Litany of the Saints is used in the liturgy (baptism and ordinations) but other devotional litanies enjoy widespread usage among Catholic Christians.

The sacred triduum of Holy Week and the nine days of prayer that intervene between Ascension Thursday and Pentecost Sunday have suggested to Christians—particularly in time of special need—the practice of a three-day or a nine-day period of insistent prayer. Those who make such tridua or novenas often use one of the following litanies as a form of supplication.

> Ask, and you shall receive;
> Seek, and you shall find;
> Knock, and the door shall be opened
>   for you   (Mt 7:7)

The Divine Praises

Blessed be God.
Blessed be his holy name.
Blessed be Jesus Christ, true God and true
    man.
Blessed be the name of Jesus.
Blessed be his most sacred heart.
Blessed be his most precious blood.
Blessed be Jesus in the most holy sacrament
    of the altar.
Blessed be the Holy Spirit, the Paraclete.
Blessed be the great mother of God, Mary
    most holy.
Blessed be her holy and immaculate
    conception.
Blessed be her glorious assumption.
Blessed be the name of Mary, virgin and
    mother.
Blessed be Saint Joseph, her most chaste
    spouse.
Blessed be God in his angels and in his
    saints.

Litany of the Holy Trinity

I

Father of Christ our Savior:
God of all consolation:
King of eternal ages:
King of the saints and angels:

Father of love and mercy:
Giver of every blessing:
—Stretch out your hand in healing.
  Save us and make us one.

II

Jesus, eternal Wisdom:
Jesus, the joy of angels:
Jesus, the Son of Mary:
Jesus, our king and shepherd:
Jesus, our priest and victim:
Jesus, our hope of glory:

—Send us your Holy Spirit,
  giver of joy and peace.

III

God the all-holy Spirit:
Bond between Son and Father:
Gift of the new creation:
Fountain of life and goodness:
Seal on God's chosen children:
Peace of the Lord's own giving:

—Lead us through grace to glory,
  one with the risen Christ.

James Quinn, S. J.

Litany to Christ Our Lord

Jesus says:
I am the bread of life.
I am the bread that came down from heaven.
If anyone eats this bread, he will live for ever
   (*Jn 6:35, 41, 51*).

—Lord, give us this bread always (*Jn 6:34*).

Jesus says:
I am the vine,
and you are the branches.
Whoever remains in me will bear much fruit,
for you can do nothing without me (*Jn 15:5*).

—Lord, we believe you are the Holy One
   who has come from God (*Jn 6:69*).

Jesus says:
I am the gate.
Whoever comes in by me will be saved (*Jn
   10:9*).

—Lord, Lord! Let us in! (*Mt 25:11*).

Jesus says:
I am the light of the world.
Whoever follows me will have the light of life
and will never walk in darkness (*Jn 8:12*).

—Send us your light and your truth (*Ps 43:3*).

Jesus says:
I am the good shepherd.

I know my sheep and they know me.
And I am willing to die for them (*Jn
 10:14–15*).

—Lord, make us one flock with one shepherd
 (*Jn 10:16*).

Jesus says:
I am the resurrection and the life.
Whoever lives and believes in me will never
 die (*Jn 11:25–26*).

—Lord, I do believe that you are the Messiah,
 the Son of God (*Jn 11:25*).

Jesus says:
I am the way, the truth and the life;
no one goes to the Father except by me (*Jn
 14:6*).

—Teach me your ways, O Lord (*Ps 25:4*).

Jesus says:
I am the one who knows everyone's thoughts
 and wishes.
I will repay each one of you according to
 what he has done (*Rv 2:22*).

—Examine me, O God, and know my heart
 (*Ps 139:27*).

Jesus says:
I am descended from the family of David;
I am the bright morning star (*Rv 22:16*).

—Son of David, have mercy on me! (*Mt 15:22*).

Jesus says:
I am the Alpha and the Omega,
the beginning and the end,
the first and the last (*Rv 22:13*).

—Lord, you show us that the first shall be
last and the last first (*Mt 19:30*).

W. G. S.

Prayer

Lord Jesus Christ,
the world's true sun,
ever rising, never setting,
whose life-giving warmth
engenders, preserves,
nourishes and gladdens
all things in heaven and on earth:
shine in my soul, I pray,
scatter the night of sin,
and the clouds of error.
Blaze within me,
that I may go my way without stumbling,
taking no part in the shameful deeds
of those who wander in the dark,
but all my life long
walking as one native to the light.
Amen.

Desiderius Erasmus (1467–1536)

Litany of the Holy Name of Jesus

Lord, have mercy.

—Lord, have mercy.

Christ, have mercy.

—Christ, have mercy.

Lord, have mercy.

—Lord have mercy.

Jesus, hear us.

—Jesus, hear and heed us.

God the Father in heaven,

—Have mercy on us.

God the Son, Redeemer of the world,
God the Holy Spirit,
Holy Trinity, one God,

Jesus, Son of the living God,
Jesus, splendor of the Father,
Jesus, brightness of eternal light,
Jesus, king of glory,
Jesus, sun of justice,
Jesus, Son of the Virgin Mary,
Jesus, worthy of all our love,
Jesus, our wonderful delight,
Jesus, mighty God,
Jesus, Father of the world to come,
Jesus, messenger of great counsel,
Jesus, most powerful,
Jesus, most patient,
Jesus, most obedient,

Jesus, gentle and humble of heart,
Jesus, lover of chastity,
Jesus, lover of the human family,
Jesus, God of peace,
Jesus, author of life,
Jesus, pattern of all virtues,
Jesus, zealous lover of souls,
Jesus, our God,
Jesus, our refuge,
Jesus, father of the poor,
Jesus, treasure of the faithful,
Jesus, good shepherd,
Jesus, true light,
Jesus, eternal wisdom,
Jesus, unbounded goodness,
Jesus, our way and our life,
Jesus, joy of angels,
Jesus, king of patriarchs,
Jesus, master of apostles,
Jesus, teacher of evangelists,
Jesus, strength of martyrs,
Jesus, light of confessors,
Jesus, purity of virgins,
Jesus, crown of all the saints,

Be merciful,

—Jesus, spare us.

Be merciful,

—Jesus, hear and heed us.

From all evil, —Jesus, deliver us.
From all sin,

From the anger of a righteous God,
From the snares of the devil,
From the spirit of uncleanness,
From everlasting death,
From neglect of your inspirations,
By the mystery of your holy incarnation,
By your birth in the stable of Bethlehem,
By your affectionate and obedient childhood,
By your divine and exemplary life,
By your labors on our behalf,
By your agony and passion,
By your cross and desolation,
By your death and burial,
By your glorious resurrection and wonderful
     ascension,
By the institution of the holy Eucharist,
By your joys and by your glory,

Lamb of God, you take away the sins of the
     world,

                    —Spare us, O Jesus.

Lamb of God, you take away the sins of the
     world,

                    —Jesus, hear and heed us.

Lamb of God, you take away the sins of the
     world,

                    —Have mercy on us, O Jesus.

Our help is in the Name of the Lord,
                    —The maker of heaven and earth.

Let us pray.

O God, our loving Father,
you appointed your Son to be the Savior of
the human race
and commanded that he should be called
Jesus.
Look with favor on us,
and grant that our respect for his holy Name
on earth
may lead to our vision of him in heaven.
We ask this through Jesus our Lord.
—Amen.

Litany of the Sacred Heart of Jesus

Lord, have mercy.

—Lord, have mercy.

Christ, have mercy.

—Christ, have mercy.

Lord, have mercy.

—Lord, have mercy.

Christ, hear us.

—Christ, graciously hear us.

God the Father in heaven,

—Have mercy on us.

God the Son, Redeemer of the world,
God the Holy Spirit,
Holy Trinity, one God,

Heart of Jesus, Son of the eternal Father,
Heart of Jesus, formed by the Holy Spirit in
the womb of the Virgin Mary,
Heart of Jesus, united with God's eternal
Word,
Heart of Jesus, of limitless majesty,
Heart of Jesus, temple of God among us,
Heart of Jesus, shrine of the Most High,
Heart of Jesus, house of God and gate of
heaven,
Heart of Jesus, glowing with love for us,
Heart of Jesus, overflowing with goodness
and love,

275

Heart of Jesus, full of kindness and love,
Heart of Jesus, fountain of all holiness,
Heart of Jesus, worthy of all praise,
Heart of Jesus, king and center of all hearts,
Heart of Jesus, treasure-house of wisdom and
knowledge,
Heart of Jesus, tabernacle of God's fullness,
Heart of Jesus, in whom the Father is
well-pleased,
Heart of Jesus, of whose fullness we have all
received,
Heart of Jesus, desire of the everlasting hills,
Heart of Jesus, patient and full of mercy,
Heart of Jesus, generous to all who turn to
you,
Heart of Jesus, source of life and holiness,
Heart of Jesus, atonement for our sins,
Heart of Jesus, overwhelmed with
reproaches,
Heart of Jesus, bruised for our sins,
Heart of Jesus, obedient all the way to death,
Heart of Jesus, pierced with a lance,
Heart of Jesus, source of all consolation,
Heart of Jesus, our life and resurrection,
Heart of Jesus, our peace and reconciliation,
Heart of Jesus, sacrifice for sin,
Heart of Jesus, salvation of all who trust in
you,
Heart of Jesus, hope of all who die in you,
Heart of Jesus, delight of all the saints,

Lamb of God, you take away the sins of the
    world,

—Spare us, O Lord.

Lamb of God, you take away the sins of the
    world,

—Graciously hear us, O Lord.

Lamb of God, you take away the sins of the
    world,

—Have mercy on us.

Jesus, gentle and humble of heart,
—Touch our hearts and make them like your
    own.

Let us pray.

Father,
we rejoice in the gifts of love
we have received from the heart of Jesus your
    Son.
Open our hearts to share his life
and continue to bless us with his love.
We ask this through our Lord Jesus Christ
    your Son,
who lives and reigns with you and the Holy
    Spirit,
one God, for ever and ever.
—Amen.

Litany to the Spirit

Come, Spirit of wisdom, and teach us to
value the highest gift.
—Come, Holy Spirit.

Come, Spirit of understanding, and show us
all things in the light of eternity.
—Come, Holy Spirit.

Come, Spirit of counsel, and guide us along
the straight and narrow path to our
heavenly home.
—Come, Holy Spirit.

Come, Spirit of might, and strengthen us
against every evil spirit and interest
which would separate us from you.
—Come, Holy Spirit.

Come, Spirit of knowledge, and teach us the
shortness of life and the length of
eternity.
—Come, Holy Spirit.

Come Spirit of godliness, and stir up our
minds and hearts to love and serve the
Lord our God all our days.
—Come, Holy Spirit.

Come, Spirit of the fear of the Lord, and
make us tremble with awe and reverence
before your divine majesty.
—Come, Holy Spirit.

Litany of Our Lady

Lord, have mercy.
—Lord, have mercy.

Christ, have mercy.
—Christ, have mercy.

Lord, have mercy.
—Lord, have mercy.

Christ, hear us.
—Christ, graciously hear us.

God the Father in heaven,
—Have mercy on us.
God the Son, Redeemer of the world,
God the Holy Spirit,
Holy Trinity, one God,

Holy Mary, —Pray for us.
Holy Mother of God,
Holy Virgin of virgins,
Mother of Christ,
Mother, full of grace,
Mother most pure,
Mother most chaste,
Immaculate Mother,
Sinless Mother,
Lovable Mother,
Model of Mothers,
Mother of good counsel,
Mother of our Maker,

279

Mother of our Savior,
Wisest of virgins,
Holiest of virgins,
Noblest of virgins,
Virgin, powerful in the sight of God,
Virgin, merciful to us sinners,
Virgin, faithful to all God asks of you,
Mirror of holiness,
Seat of wisdom,
Cause of our joy,
Shrine of the Spirit,
Honor of your people,
Devoted handmaid of the Lord,
Mystical rose,
Tower of David,
Tower of ivory,
House of gold,
Ark of the covenant,
Gate of heaven,
Star of hope,
Health of the sick,
Refuge of sinners,
Comfort of the afflicted,
Help of Christians,
Queen of angels,
Queen of patriarchs,
Queen of prophets,
Queen of apostles,
Queen of martyrs,
Queen of confessors,
Queen of virgins,

Queen of all saints,
Queen conceived in holiness,
Queen raised up to glory,
Queen of the rosary,
Queen of peace,

Lamb of God, you take away the sins of the
world,

—Spare us, O Lord.

Lamb of God, you take away the sins of the
world,

—Graciously hear us, O Lord.

Lamb of God, you take away the sins of the
world,

—Have mercy on us.

Pray for us, O holy Mother of God,
—That we may be made worthy of the
promises of Christ.

Let us pray.

Lord God,
give to your people the joy
of continual health in mind and body.
With the prayers of the Virgin Mary to help
us,
guide us through the sorrows of this life
to eternal happiness in the life to come.
We ask this through Christ our Lord.
—Amen.

Litany of St. Joseph

Lord, have mercy.

—Lord, have mercy.

Christ, have mercy.

—Christ have mercy,

Lord, have mercy.

—Lord, have mercy.

Christ, hear us.

—Christ, graciously hear us.

God the Father in heaven,

—Have mercy on us.

God the Son, Redeemer of the world,
God the Holy Spirit,
Holy Trinity, one God,

St. Joseph,   —Pray for us.
Renowned scion of David,
Light of patriarchs,
Husband of the Mother of God,
Chaste guardian of the Virgin,
Foster-father of the Son of God,
Watchful defender of Christ,
Head of the holy family,
Joseph, most just,
Joseph, most pure,
Joseph, most prudent,
Joseph, most valiant,
Joseph, most obedient,
Joseph most faithful,
Mirror of patience,
Lover of poverty,

Model of artisans,
Glory of domestic life,
Guardian of virgins,
Mainstay of families,
Consolation of those in trouble,
Hope of the sick,
Patron of the dying,
Terror of demons,
Protector of holy Church.

Lamb of God, you take away the sins of the
world,

—Spare us, O Lord.
Lamb of God, you take away the sins of the
world,

—Graciously hear us, O Lord.
Lamb of God, you take away the sins of the
world,

—Have mercy on us.
He made him lord of his household,
—And ruler over all his possessions.

Let us pray.

God,
in your infinite wisdom and love
you chose Joseph to be the husband of Mary,
the mother of your Son.
May we have the help of his prayers in
heaven
and enjoy his protection on earth.
We ask this through Christ our Lord.
—Amen.

Litany of the Saints

God our Father in heaven,
                    —Have mercy on us.
God the Son, our Redeemer,
God the Holy Spirit,
Holy Trinity, one God,

Holy Mary,   —Pray for us.
Mother of God,
Most honored of all virgins,
Michael, Gabriel and Raphael,
Angels of God,

Abraham, Moses and Elijah,
Saint John the Baptist,
Saint Joseph,
Holy patriarchs and prophets,

Saint Peter and Saint Paul,
Saint Andrew,
Saint John and Saint James,
Saint Thomas,
Saint Matthew,
All holy Apostles,

Saint Luke,
Saint Mark,
Saint Barnabas,
Saint Mary Magdalene,
All disciples of the Lord,

Saint Stephen,
Saint Ignatius,
Saint Polycarp,
Saint Justin,
Saint Lawrence,
Saint Cyprian,
Saint Boniface,
Saint Stanislaus,
Saint Thomas Becket,
Saint John Fisher and Saint Thomas More,
Saint Paul Miki,
Saint Isaac Jogues and Saint John de Brebeuf,
Saint Peter Chanel,
Saint Charles Lwanga,
Saint Perpetua and Saint Felicity,
Saint Agnes,
Saint Maria Goretti,
All holy martyrs for Christ,

Saint Leo and Saint Gregory,
Saint Ambrose,
Saint Jerome,
Saint Augustine,
Saint Athanasius,
Saint Basil and Saint Gregory,
Saint John Chrysostom,

Saint Martin,
Saint Patrick,
Saint Cyril and Saint Methodius,
Saint Charles Borromeo,
Saint Francis de Sales,
Saint Pius,
Saint Anthony,
Saint Benedict,
Saint Bernard,
Saint Francis and Saint Dominic,
Saint Thomas Aquinas,
Saint Ignatius Loyola,
Saint Francis Xavier,
Saint Vincent de Paul,
Saint John Vianney,
Saint John Bosco,
Saint Catherine,
Saint Teresa,
Saint Rose,
Saint Louis,
Saint Monica,
Saint Elizabeth,
All holy men and women,

Christ, Son of the living God,
     —Have mercy on us.

You came into this world,
You suffered for us on the cross,
You died to save us,
You lay in the tomb,
You rose from the dead,

You returned in glory to the Father,
You sent the Holy Spirit upon your Apostles,
You are seated at the right hand of the
    Father,
You will come again to judge the living and
    the dead,

Lord, show us your kindness,
                  —Lord, hear our prayer.
Raise our thoughts and desires to you,
Save us from final damnation,
Save our friends and all who have helped us,
Grant eternal rest to all who have died in the
    faith,
Spare us from disease, hunger and war,
Bring all peoples together in trust and peace,
Guide and protect your holy Church,
Keep the Pope and all the clergy
  in faithful service to your Church,
Bring all Christians together in unity,
Lead all peoples to the light of the gospel,

Lamb of God, you take away the sins of the
    world,
                  —Have mercy on us.

Lamb of God, you take away the sins of the
    world,
                  —Have mercy on us.

Lamb of God, you take away the sins of the
    world,
                  —Have mercy on us.

Let us pray.

God of love, our strength and protection,
hear the prayers of your Church.
Grant that when we come to you in faith,
our prayers may be answered,
through Christ our Lord.
—Amen.

Prayer does not blind us to the world, but it
transforms our vision of the world, and
makes us see it, all men, and all the
history of mankind, in the light of God.

Thomas Merton

7. Eucharistic Devotions

THE LORD'S SUPPER on the Lord's Day is the central liturgical action of God's people. In the eucharistic celebration we listen as God speaks to us in the bible readings and the homily; we pray for our needs, general and particular; and we praise and thank our heavenly Father for all that he has done for us in Christ, for all that he is doing for us this very day, and for all that he promises to do for us in the days to come. We ratify and complete all this by eating and drinking his sacramental body and blood in a holy communion: "the gifts of God for the people of God."

This communal act of worship and dedication is prolonged, so to speak, in the sacrament reserved primarily for the sick and dying (*viaticum*). Over the centuries the tabernacle has become the focus of many forms of devotion, reminding us continually of Jesus' abiding presence with his Church and extending the grace of the sacrifice to all the hours of the day and night.

The prayers included here may be used before or after Mass or for private visits to the Blessed Sacrament. The Hours of the Blessed Sacrament (pages 142–151) would also be suitable for visits.

Hymn to the Blessed Sacrament

Godhead here in hiding, whom I do adore
Masked by these bare shadows, shape and
    nothing more,
See, Lord, at thy service low lies here a heart
Lost, all lost in wonder at the God thou art.

Seeing, touching, tasting are in thee
    deceived;
How says trusty hearing? That shall be
    believed;
What God's Son has told me, take for truth I
    do;
Truth himself speaks truly or there's nothing
    true.

On the cross thy godhead made no sign to
    men;
Here thy very manhood steals from human
    ken:
Both are my confession, both are my belief,
And I pray the prayer of the dying thief.

I am not like Thomas, wounds I cannot see,
But can plainly call thee Lord and God as he:
This faith each day deeper be my holding of,
Daily make me harder hope and dearer love.

O thou our reminder of Christ crucified,
Living Bread the life of us for whom he died,
Lend this life to me then: feed and feast my
    mind,
There be thou the sweetness man was meant
    to find.

Bring the tender tale true of the Pelican;
Bathe me, Jesu Lord, in what thy bosom
    ran—
Blood that but one drop of has the world to
    win
All the world forgiveness of its world of sin.

Jesu whom I look at shrouded here below,
I beseech thee send me what I thirst for so,
Some day to gaze on thee face to face in light
And be blest for ever with thy glory's sight.

St. Thomas Aquinas (1225–1274)
Adoro Te Devote
Trans. Gerard Manley Hopkins

Sing, My Tongue, the Savior's Glory

Hail our Savior's glorious Body,
Which his Virgin Mother bore;
Hail the Blood which, shed for sinners,
Did a broken world restore;
Hail the sacrament most holy,
Flesh and Blood of Christ adore!

To the Virgin, for man's healing,
His own Son the Father sends;
From the Father's love proceeding
Sower, seed and Word descends;
Wondrous life of Word incarnate
With his greatest wonder ends!

On that paschal evening see him
With the chosen twelve recline,
To the old law still obedient
In its feast of love divine;
Love divine, the new law giving,
Gives himself as Bread and Wine!

By his word the Word almighty
Makes of bread his flesh indeed;
Wine becomes his very life-blood:
Faith God's living Word must heed!
Faith alone may safely guide us
Where the senses cannot lead!

Come, adore this wondrous presence;
Bow to Christ, the source of grace!
Here is kept the ancient promise
Of God's earthly dwelling-place!
Sight is blind before God's glory,
Faith alone may see his face!

Glory be to God the Father,
Praise to his co-equal Son,
Adoration to the Spirit,
Bond of love, in Godhead one!
Blest be God by all creation
Joyously while ages run!

St. Thomas Aquinas (1225–1274)
Pange Lingua Gloriosi
Trans. James Quinn, S.J.

Prayer Before Mass

Almighty and ever-living God,
I approach the sacrament of your
    only-begotten Son, our Lord Jesus
    Christ.
I come unclean to the fountain of mercy,
blind to the radiance of eternal light,
poor and needy to the Lord of heaven and
    earth.
Lord, in your great generosity,
heal my sickness, wash away my defilement,
enlighten my blindness, enrich my poverty,
and clothe my nakedness.
May I receive the bread of angels,

the King of kings and Lord of lords,
with humble reverence,
with the purity and faith,
the repentence and love, and the determined
      purpose
that will help to bring me to salvation.
May I receive the sacrament of the Lord's
      body and blood,
and its reality and power.
Kind God,
may I receive the body of your only-begotten
      Son, our Lord Jesus Christ,
born from the womb of the Virgin Mary,
and so be received into his mystical body,
and numbered among his members.
Loving Father,
as on my earthly pilgrimage
I now receive your beloved Son
under the veil of a sacrament,
may I one day see him face to face in glory,
who lives and reigns with you for ever.
Amen.

St. Thomas Aquinas (1225–1274)

In every human being there is an abyss that
      only God can fill.

Blaise Pascal

Prayer After Mass

Lord, Father all-powerful, and ever-living
    God, I thank you,
for even though I am a sinner, your
    unprofitable servant,
not because of my worth, but in the kindness
    of your mercy,
you have fed me
with the precious body and blood of your
    Son, our Lord Jesus Christ.
I pray that this holy communion
may not bring me condemnation and
    punishment
but forgiveness and salvation.
May it be a helmet of faith
and a shield of good will.
May it purify me from evil ways
and put an end to my evil passions.
May it bring me charity and patience,
humility and obedience,
and growth in the power to do good.
May it be my strong defense
against all my enemies, visible and invisible,
and the perfect calming of all my evil
    impulses,
bodily and spiritual.
May it unite me more closely to you,
the one true God,
and lead me safely through death
to everlasting happiness with you.
And I pray that you will lead me, a sinner,

to the banquet where you,
with your Son and Holy Spirit,
are true and perfect light,
total fulfillment, everlasting joy,
gladness without end,
and perfect happiness to your saints.
Grant this through Christ our Lord.
Amen.

St. Thomas Aquinas (1225–1274)

Jesus Our Delight

Jesus to cast one thought upon
Makes gladness after he is gone;
But more than honey and honeycomb
Is to come near and take him home.

Song never was so sweet in ear,
Word never was such news to hear,
Thought half so sweet there is not one
As Jesus God the Father's Son.

Jesu, their hope who go astray,
So kind to those who ask the way,
So good to those who look for Thee,
To those who find what must Thou be?

To speak of that no tongue will do
Nor letters suit to spell it true;
But they can guess who have tasted of
What Jesus is and what is love.

Jesu, a springing well thou art,
Daylight to head and treat to heart,
And matched with thee there's nothing glad
That men have wished for or have had.

Wish us good morning when we wake
And light us, Lord, with thy day-break.
Beat from our brains the thicky night
And fill the world up with delight.

Be our delight, O Jesu, now
As by and by our prize art thou,
And grant our glorying may be
World without end alone in thee.

Jesu Dulcis Memoria
12th century hymn
Trans. Gerard Manley Hopkins

How Holy This Feast!

How holy this feast in which Christ is our
    food;
his passion is recalled;
grace fills our hearts;
and we receive a pledge of the glory to come.

I am the living bread come down from
    heaven.
—Anyone who eats this bread will live for
    ever.

Let us pray.

Lord Jesus Christ,

you gave us the Eucharist
as the memorial of your suffering and death.
May our worship of this sacrament of your
    body and blood
help us to experience the salvation you won
    for us
and the peace of the kingdom,
where you live with the Father and the Holy
    Spirit,
one God, for ever and ever.
—Amen.

Lord Jesus Christ,
we worship you living among us
in the sacrament of your body and blood.
May we offer to our Father in heaven
a solemn pledge of undivided love.
May we offer to our brothers and sisters
a life poured out in loving service of that
    kingdom,
where you live with the Father and the Holy
    Spirit,
one God, for ever and ever.
—Amen.

Almighty God,
we offer you our souls and bodies
to be a living sacrifice
through Jesus Christ our Lord.
Send us into the world in the power of your
    Spirit,
to live and work for your praise and glory.
—Amen.

To Jesus Living in Mary

Jesu that dost in Mary dwell,
Be in thy servants' hearts as well,
In the spirit of thy holiness,
In the fullness of thy force and stress,
In the very ways that thy life goes,
And virtues that thy pattern shows,
In the sharing of thy mysteries;
And every power in us that is
Against thy power put under feet
In the Holy Ghost the Paraclete
To the glory of the Father. Amen.

Fr. Charles de Condren (1588–1641)
Trans. Gerard Manley Hopkins

O God I Love Thee

O God, I love thee, I love thee—
Not out of hope of heaven for me
Nor fearing not to love and be
  In the everlasting burning.
Thou, thou, my Jesus, after me
  Didst reach thine arms out dying,
For my sake sufferedst nails and lance,
Mocked and marrèd countenance,
  Sorrows passing number,
  Sweat and care and cumber,
Yea and death, and this for me,
  And thou couldst see me sinning:
Then I, why should not I love thee,
Jesu, so much in love with me?

Not for heaven's sake; not to be
Out of hell by loving thee;
Not for any gains I see;
But just the way that thou didst me
I do love and I will love thee:
What must I love thee, Lord, for then?
For being my king and God. Amen.

St. Francis Xavier (1506–1552)
O Deus, Ego Amo Te
Trans. Gerard Manley Hopkins

Prayer to Our Redeemer

Soul of Christ, make me holy,
Body of Christ, be my salvation.
Blood of Christ, let me drink your wine.
Water flowing from the side of Christ, wash
    me clean.
Passion of Christ strengthen me.
Kind Jesus, hear my prayer;
hide me within your wounds
and keep me close to you.
Defend me from the evil enemy.
Call me at my death
to the fellowship of your saints,
that I may sing your praise with them
through all eternity. Amen.

Prayer of Self-Dedication to Jesus Christ

Lord Jesus Christ,
take all my freedom,
my memory, my understanding, and my
    will.
All that I have and cherish
you have given me.
I surrender it all to be guided by your will.
Your grace and your love
are wealth enough for me.
Give me these, Lord Jesus,
and I ask for nothing more.

Prayer to Jesus Christ Crucified

My good and dear Jesus,
I kneel before you,
asking you most earnestly
to engrave upon my heart
a deep and lively faith, hope, and charity,
with true repentence for my sins,
and a firm resolve to make amends.
As I reflect upon your five wounds,
and dwell upon them with deep compassion
    and grief,
I recall, good Jesus, the words the prophet
    David spoke
long ago concerning you:
they have pierced my hands and my feet,
they have counted all my bones!

Let your prayer be completely simple, for
    both the Publican and the Prodigal Son
    were reconciled to God by a single
    phrase.

John Climacus

8. Reconciliation

"REPENT AND BELIEVE the Good News" (*Mk 1:15*).

We know we are sinners. Therefore, we seek reconciliation with God and with one another. This entails a radical transformation of our lives—a long process of growth from selfishness to generosity.

The Sacrament of Penance is an important way to stimulate this growth. By its emphasis on reconciliation and forgiveness, the new Rite of Penance has already proved its worth.

Apart from occasions when we receive this sacrament we need times when we can look carefully at our lives privately. We discern the Lord's presence there and illuminate the dark side where we have failed to live his law of love.

We can use the following section for help in making this prayerful exploration. Or we may use it to prepare for a devout reception of the Sacrament of Penance.

Prayer to the Holy Spirit

Come, O Holy Spirit, come.
Come as the wind and cleanse;
come as the fire and burn;
convert and consecrate our lives
to our great good and your great glory;
through Jesus Christ our Lord.

Scripture Readings

Matthew 9: 9–13   As he passed on from there Jesus saw a man named Matthew at his seat in the custom-house, and said to him, "Follow me"; and Matthew rose and followed him. When Jesus was at table in the house, many bad characters—tax-gatherers and others—were seated with him and his disciples. The Pharisees noticed this, and said to his disciples, "Why is it that your master eats with tax-gatherers and sinners?" Jesus heard it and said, "It is not the healthy that need a doctor, but the sick. Go and learn what that text means, 'I require mercy, not sacrifice.' I did not come to invite virtuous people, but sinners." (NEB)

Luke 15: 1–10 Another time, the tax-gatherers and other bad characters were all crowding in to listen to him; and the Pharisees and the doctors of the law began grumbling among themselves: "This fellow," they said, "welcomes sinners and eats with them." He answered them with this parable: "If one of you has a hundred sheep and loses one of them, does he not leave the ninety-nine in the open pasture and go after the missing one until he has found it? How delighted he is then! He lifts it on to his shoulders, and home he goes to call his friends and neighbors together. 'Rejoice with me!' he cries. 'I have found my lost sheep.' In the same way, I tell you, there will be greater joy in heaven over one sinner who repents than over ninety-nine righteous people who do not need to repent.

"Or again, if a woman has ten silver pieces and loses one of them, does she not light the lamp, sweep out the house, and look in every corner till she has found it? And when she has, she calls her friends and neighbors together, and says, 'Rejoice with me! I have found the piece that I lost.' In the same way, I tell you, there is joy among the angels of God over one sinner who repents." (NEB)

John 20:19–23 Late that Sunday evening, when the disciples were together behind locked doors, for fear of the Jews, Jesus came and stood among them. "Peace be with you!" he said, and then showed them his hands and his side. So when the disciples saw the Lord, they were filled with joy. Jesus repeated, "Peace be with you!" and said, "As the Father sent me, so I send you." Then he breathed on them, saying, "Receive the Holy Spirit! If you forgive anyone's sins, they stand forgiven; if you pronounce them unforgiven, unforgiven they remain." (NEB)

Reflect on any or all of these passages for a short time, recalling the great love and forgiveness which the Father has graciously extended to us during our lives. He continues to offer us this forgiveness and asks us to be reconciled with him and with our neighbor. There are many other passages in scripture which can also be used, among them the following:

Luke	5: 17–26	Christ Forgives and Cures the Paralytic.
Luke	7: 36–50	The Lord and a Penitent Woman
Luke	15: 11–32	The Wandering and Wasteful Son Who Returned Home
Luke	19: 1–10	Jesus and Zacchaeus the Tax Collector
John	8: 1–11	A Woman Caught in Adultery

Guidelines From Scripture

The Old Law

The Ten Commandments (Ex 20: 2–17)

1. I, the Lord, am your God. You shall not have other gods besides me.
2. You shall not take the name of the Lord, your God, in vain.
3. Remember to keep holy the sabbath day.
4. Honor your father and your mother.
5. You shall not kill.
6. You shall not commit adultery.
7. You shall not steal.
8. You shall not bear false witness against your neighbor.
9. You shall not covet your neighbor's wife.
10. You shall not covet anything that belongs to your neighbor.

The New Law

The Great Commandment (Mk 12: 28–31)

Then one of the lawyers, who had been listening to these discussions and had noted how well he answered, came forward and asked him, "Which commandment is first of all?" Jesus answered, "The first is, 'Hear, O Israel: the Lord our God is the only Lord; love the Lord your God with all your heart, with all your soul, with all your mind, and with all your strength.' The second is this: 'Love your neighbor as yourself.' There is no other commandment greater than these." (NEB)

The New Commandment (Jn 13: 34–35)

"I give you a new commandment: love one another; as I have loved you, so you are to love one another. If there is this love among you, then all will know that you are my disciples." (NEB)

The Beatitudes (Mt 5: 3–10)

1. How blest are those who know their need of God; the kingdom of heaven is theirs.
2. How blest are the sorrowful; they shall find consolation.
3. How blest are those of a gentle spirit; they shall have the earth for their possession.
4. How blest are those who hunger and thirst to see right prevail; they shall be satisfied.
5. How blest are those who show mercy; mercy shall be shown to them.
6. How blest are those whose hearts are pure; they shall see God.
7. How blest are the peacemakers; God shall call them his sons.
8. How blest are those who have suffered persecution for the cause of right; the kingdom of Heaven is theirs. (NEB)

Examination of Conscience

To sin is to break a bond, to destroy a relationship, to withdraw myself from God, my Father, and from his love.... A sinful act is less important for the disorder it creates than for what it says about me as a person: Who am I? Whom do I love? What is my attitude toward God?

W. J. Burghardt, S.J.

  I. *The Lord says: "Love the Lord your God with your whole heart."*

Do I keep God in mind and put him first in my life? Or am I too caught up in material concerns?

Do I worship God regularly and carefully?

Do I respect his name, or have I dishonored it by using it in anger and carelessness?

Do I try to grow in my understanding of the faith?

Do I pray even when I don't feel like it?

Do I trust God and take seriously enough his personal love and concern for me?

Do I genuinely repent of my sins and accept God's free and gracious forgiveness?

II. *The Lord says: "Love one another as I have loved you."*

Do I love my family and try to create a happy home life? Or am I sometimes thoughtless and even cruel toward them?

Do I try to maintain and foster friendships and give genuine respect and support to other people?

Am I fair and honest in my relationships? Or do I sometimes lie or take unfair advantage of others by cheating them or stealing from them?

Do I respect the rights and sensitivities of others? Or do I tend to categorize people unfairly or ignore them because they are different?

Do I honestly try to forgive people who dislike me? Or have I tried to hurt them by what I've said or done?

Am I trying to improve the quality of life around me? Or do I foul up the environment and waste the good things I have?

Do I really care about my country and the good of the human community of which I am a part? Or do I care only about myself and the people I know?

Am I concerned for the poor, the hungry and the destitute and for the millions who thirst for justice and peace?

Can I contribute more of my time, talents and money to the poor of the world?

III. *Jesus says: "Be perfect as your heavenly Father is perfect."*

Am I working at becoming a better person and a better Christian?

Am I making the most of my talents, my education and my opportunities? Or do I fail to use them sometimes?

Do I take care of my body, and make sure I get enough sleep and exercise? Do I eat and drink in moderation?

Am I grateful for my sexuality and anxious to grow in sexual maturity and responsibility? Or do I misuse my sexual powers in selfish or exploitative ways?

Am I able to admit my own need for help and to ask for it?

Do I accept myself, despite my limitations and weakness?

What is the fundamental orientation of my life?

Prayers of Sorrow and Thanksgiving

Reflection on the following prayers, or others in this book (cf. especially the Prayer for All Seasons section, pp. 29–83) can make us more aware of our need for sorrow . . . and more grateful to God for the forgiveness which he offers us unceasingly.

Listen to My Prayer

Lord Jesus,
you opened the eyes of the blind,
healed the sick,
forgave the sinful woman,
and after Peter's denial confirmed him in
　　　your love.
Listen to my prayer:
forgive all my sins,
renew your love in my heart,
help me to live in perfect unity with my
　　　fellow Christians
that I may proclaim your saving power to all
　　　the world.

Fill Our Hearts With Faith

Lord God,
creator and ruler of your kingdom of light,
in your great love for this world
you gave up your only Son
for our salvation.
His cross has redeemed us,
his death has given us life,

his resurrection has raised us to glory.
Through him we ask you
to be always present among your family.
Teach us to be reverent in the presence of
    your glory;
fill our hearts with faith,
our days with good works,
our lives with your love;
may your truth be on our lips
and your wisdom in all our actions,
that we may receive the reward of everlasting
    life.
We ask this through Christ our Lord.

Bless the Lord

(Ps 103:1 4, 8–18)

Bless the Lord, O my soul;
    and all my being, bless his holy name.
Bless the Lord, O my soul,
    and forget not all his benefits;
He pardons all your iniquities,
    he heals all your ills.
He redeems your life from destruction,
    he crowns you with kindness and
        compassion.
Merciful and gracious is the Lord,
    slow to anger and abounding in kindness.

He will not always chide,
  nor does he keep his wrath forever.
Not according to our sins does he deal with
    us,
  nor does he requite us according to our
    crimes.
For as the heavens are high above the earth,
  so surpassing is his kindness toward those
    who fear him.

As far as the east is from the west,
  so far has he put our transgressions from
    us.
As a father has compassion on his children,
  so the Lord has compassion on those who
    fear him,
For he knows how we are formed;
  he remembers that we are dust.

Man's days are like those of grass;
  like a flower of the field he blooms;
The wind sweeps over him and he is gone,
  and his place knows him no more.
But the kindness of the Lord is from eternity
  to eternity toward those who fear him,
And his justice toward children's children
  among those who keep his covenant
  and remember to fulfill his precepts.

(NAB)

9. Meditative Prayer

AFTER A LONG DAY of preaching and healing,
the Gospels tell us, Jesus would go off by himself and pray to his Father. What was this
prayer like? It must have been an intimate
sharing with his Father, a sharing which included praise, thanksgiving, and an urgent
plea for guidance to understand and carry out
his mission.

We also have a similar need to share inti-
mately with the Father as well as with the
Risen Lord himself. Harried and scattered as
we are by the frenetic pace of our lives, we
need to be refreshed by prayerful reflection in
solitude. This is what we mean by the term
"meditative prayer."

Too often we think that meditative prayer
is a luxury reserved for monks and mystics.
Not so. More and more Christians are realiz-
ing that they not only are called on to spend
time daily in meditative prayer, but also are

finding that this prayer helps them grow steadily in their union with God.

Where to begin? Reflection on a passage in the bible is an obvious possibility. For example, consider the following passage from the 12th chapter of Luke's Gospel:

Then he said to his disciples, "This is why I am telling you not to worry about your life and what you are to eat, nor about your body and how you are to clothe it. For life means more than food and the body more than clothing. Think of the ravens. They do not sow or reap; they have no storehouses and no barns; yet God feeds them. And how much more are you worth than the birds! (Lk. 12, 22–25). (JB)

We know that Jesus intended those words not only for his listeners on that day but for the millions who would hear and read them down through the centuries. In a deeply personal way he directs those words to you and me.

With this in mind, we read over the passage two or three times and ask the Lord to enlighten us. What does he want us to hear today as we once more dwell on these familiar words? As we try to answer that question we are drawn into a very personal application of that passage to our lives. Our reflection would not be spoken aloud, much less written down; but if it were jotted down later it might come out looking like this:

"Lord, once more I read these words and I realize that I am caught up in all sorts of worries. Worries about my family, my job, my health. Are you telling me to relax and trust more in you? I think you are. Lord, I praise and thank you for pledging yourself to take care of me and the people I love. How great it is to hear that you regard me as a valuable person, and love me! I rejoice, too, at the beautiful picture you give me of the ravens. Outside my window now I see countless beauties of nature which come from the Father. I hear birds outside who, like the ravens, are not sowing or reaping but simply are *living*! And Lord, you do feed them, don't you?

"Nevertheless, Lord, you'll forgive me if I simply call your attention to the needs I have, trusting that you will take care of them as you take care of the birds. I'm thinking of that operation which my mother faces next week and our bank account which was never lower.

"Lord, I praise and thank you and promise to trust in you throughout this busy day. Help me to make this passage live today in my heart and in my life."

Depending on our mood and the inspiration of the Spirit, the reflection might take this course; or it might go in a completely different direction. In any event, the passage could well provide food for meditative prayer for a few minutes or a much longer time. The important point is that we would be making that bible passage part of ourselves and seeking to enflesh it in our lives. Thus does the Lord speak to us!

Sometimes a simple phrase from scripture can trigger a deep experience of meditative prayer. "Young man, I tell you to get up," Jesus says to the dead young man of Nain (Lk 7:15). How easy for a young man (or young woman) today to identify with that command! The meditation might go like this:

"Lord, I am a lot like that young man. True, I'm not dead physically. Nor am I dead spiritually either, as far as I know—I'm not the world's greatest sinner or anything like that! But I am so selfish and self-centered that it amazes me at times. Like the young man, I too need to be *raised up*. Help me to be more aware of my parents and brothers and sisters; help me to be more sensitive to the moods of my friends."

Nudged by the Lord, the young person might then become much more specific about virtues such as courage and patience which he or she needs in great supply at that particular moment. Or the meditation might take a different turn suggested by the Lord. In any event it could be a rich experience of prayer touched off by a single phrase.

To take another example, who can fail to see himself or herself in Cleopas and his companion? On their way to Emmaus, they journeyed for some time with a mysterious stranger and never guessed he was the Risen Lord until they broke bread with him. Afterwards, they puzzled over their blindness: "Did not our hearts burn within us as he talked to us on the road and explained the scriptures to us?" (Lk 24: 32).

Struck by that remark, we might find ourselves meditating on how we are equally blind. "How often, Lord," we might reflect to ourselves, "have I failed to see you in the most obvious places—for example in the features of my own family? I need special help to see you in those close to me, especially when they get on my nerves like they did yesterday. For that matter I need to see you also in those who are not close to me at all—that poor old woman I passed by so quickly today on my way home from town."

Meditating on this incident and the outcry of the two men might open us to the call of the Lord. He is always challenging us to be more alert to his presence in precisely those persons in whom we have the greatest trouble locating him.

In short, by spending time daily in reflection on the Gospels, Psalms, letters of Paul, etc. we gradually come more and more in contact with God and apply his word more and more to our lives. Scripture is a storehouse of riches for meditative prayer.

But reflection on a passage in the bible is not the only entry to meditative prayer. One of the oldest and simplest ways is the Jesus Prayer, which can be traced back to the early centuries of the Church. By repeatedly invoking the name of Jesus, Christians find they can penetrate deeply into the presence of God who saves and sanctifies. The name of Jesus is sometimes repeated by itself or inserted in a phrase like—

> Lord Jesus Christ
> Son of the living God,
> have mercy on me, a sinner.

The best way to say the Jesus prayer is to sit in as much physical and inner stillness as we can manage and to repeat the invocation over and over, slowly and insistently. We fix our attention directly on the words of the prayer itself, without trying to form images or ideas. In a way we thus "clear away" the concerns which occupy our every waking moment, and allow the Lord to speak to us. As we pronounce the name of Jesus with deep reverence and faith, we bring his presence and power into our lives.

Many Christians spend a definite period of time each day on the Jesus Prayer and find that it becomes the very substance of their prayer life. For them, it is much more than a mechanical repetition of a word or phrase; it is a practice of meditative prayer which leads to a deep union with Jesus and with his Father.

A similar entry to meditative prayer is described in *The Cloud of Unknowing,* a book by an anonymous English Catholic writer of the 14th century. Called "the centering prayer" by some, this simple method resembles the Jesus Prayer but comes out of a different time and tradition. We find a quiet place and sit comfortably with our eyes closed. We center all our attention and desire on God dwelling within us, turning ourselves over to him, and remaining quietly in his presence. Then we respond to God's presence with a single word like "God" or "love" and let this word repeat itself within us, focusing on the word and not trying to summon up ideas or images.

Whenever we become aware of distractions, we calmly turn back to the prayer word and continue to abide in God's presence. At the end of 20 minutes or so, we conclude with an Our Father which is said slowly and reflectively.

Like those who use the Jesus Prayer, Christians who are drawn to the centering prayer frequently find that their union with God has deepened immensely. They discover a dimension to prayer which has eluded them until then.

Scripture reflection, the Jesus Prayer or the centering prayer of *The Cloud of Unknowing*—these are practical approaches to meditative prayer. Others meditate by saying very slowly classic prayers such as the Lord's Prayer or the Creed, or by means of such devotions as the Rosary or the Way of the Cross. Still others will find material for reflection in some prayers in this book.

For example, a wealth of material may be found in The Year of Our Lord (pp. 183–242) and The Week with Christ (pp. 85–182). A particular psalm, poem or prayer in those sections may trigger a period of meditative prayer for us. Or the Lord may use some other section in the book to get his message across to us—one of the familiar Prayers for Everyday (pp. 15–28), for instance, or one of the Prayers for All Seasons (pp. 29–83). Those praying the Jesus Prayer will find sustenance in several of the litanies (pp. 268–277).

No matter what the approach we favor, or where we look for material for reflection, we are urged to spend a certain period of time daily at meditative prayer. Generally, it is far better to spend five minutes a day *each* day than a half-hour one day and nothing the next. Most of us find it convenient to set aside a particular time daily, perhaps early in the morning or just before bed at night. It is also a good idea to set aside a certain place, a "prayer nook" which is accessible even when privacy is at a premium. Finally, we must remind ourselves that sometimes we will feel the time we spend is utterly wasted— "Nothing is happening!" At those times we must simply wait on the Lord in patience and trust. After all, the work of prayer is not really our work but his, and if he should wish to give us times of dryness that's his business and not ours.

Such times of dryness will not last long. The Lord is a gracious giver and will not be surpassed in generosity. As we set aside time and space for meditative prayer we will find him drawing closer to us and lighting up our lives in ways we never imagined.

Let us meditate on the Gospels. Amidst the confusion of so many human words, the Gospel is the only voice that enlightens and attracts, that consoles and quenches thirst.

Pope John XXIII

10. Way of the Cross

OVER THE CENTURIES, the Way of the Cross has been a meaningful devotion for many Christians. They have found value in reflecting on the passion, death and resurrection of the Lord by isolating various episodes which occurred after his arrest in the Garden.

In our own day, many believe that the Way of the Cross has just as much meaning as it ever did—perhaps even more! Certainly there is no shortage of suffering in this world of ours: the Way of the Cross continues in the suffering of humanity.

The Way of the Cross which follows is primarily for private use. We can use it in the privacy of our homes or, perhaps better, in a church or chapel where there are stations on the walls which depict these episodes.

First Station: Jesus Is Condemned to Death

A weak and unscrupulous judge sentences an innocent man to death. Jesus, whose only "crime" was his loving care for all he met, is marked for execution with two common criminals.

Injustice is not limited to this specific case long ago in a distant city. We know that millions today suffer from injustice of one kind or other. As in the days of Jesus, courts and judges sometimes do not advance the cause of justice but make matters worse.

Prayer

Lord, I too sometimes feel "condemned"... sentenced to a life which I never really anticipated. Things seldom have worked out the way I hoped and planned. Help me to see your plan in my life even if it is different from my own. Help me to realize that you indeed "write straight with crooked lines."

Our Father. Hail Mary. Glory.

Second Station: Jesus Accepts His Cross

After beating and mocking Jesus, the soldiers present him with the instrument of his impending destruction—the cross. He accepts it with love.

The cross is a symbol for today's world. How many millions are forced to bear the cross of injustice, poverty and war while the rest of us look on without lifting a finger to help them. We must not lay guilt on ourselves; but we must be aware of the complacency which numbs our consciences.

Prayer

Lord, I have lived long enough to see the deaths of good friends and family members I loved dearly. Without being maudlin, I know that the days ahead will reveal other crosses which you will ask me to bear. Help me to accept them with calm and hope, knowing that you hold me as firmly as you once held the cross you carried.

Our Father. Hail Mary. Glory.

Third Station: Jesus Falls the First Time

The long journey to Calvary begins. Suddenly his legs buckle under the weight of the cross, and Jesus slumps to the ground.

The weakness and fall of Jesus were caused by the inhuman treatment he received from his captors. Just as humiliating, however, is the weakness suffered by the elderly who fall beneath the weight of their years and ills. Yet, often are they overlooked and left to languish and die in isolation.

Prayer

Lord, I thank you for the health you have given me and the fact that I can praise you this day. I am very grateful. Please help me to be more sensitive to the needs of the older persons in my life and protect me from a joyless old age when my powers fail.

Our Father. Hail Mary. Glory.

Fourth Station: Jesus Meets His Mother

As Jesus is shoved toward the hill of death, he suddenly comes face-to-face with his mother. It is a poignant encounter for both.

Few things affect us more deeply than the love of a mother for a suffering son or daughter. All her love and life and hopes for the future are centered on that troubled young person. How often in our day are mothers brought face-to-face with children ruined by wars or by self-inflicted disasters like drug addiction!

Prayer

Lord, I praise you and thank you for the young persons whom you have allowed to enter my life. When they get on my nerves and upset me, please help me realize that this is a small price to pay for their presence. May Mary love them with the same love she showed you during your years together on earth.

Our Father. Hail Mary. Glory.

Fifth Station: Simon Helps Jesus Carry the Cross

When the soldiers realized that Jesus would never reach Calvary without help, they conscripted Simon to carry the cross.

Simon came forward reluctantly, dragging his feet. Nor can we blame him. We, too, turn away from tragedy. Who wants to get involved? And so tragedy's victims suffer on and on.

Prayer

Lord, I find myself caught up too often in my own private world of unpaid bills and minor sicknesses. It's so easy to wall myself off from the world. Help me to realize that there are many outside those walls who have crosses which I can help them carry, and "conscript" me for the task if necessary.

Our Father. Hail Mary. Glory.

Sixth Station: Veronica Wipes the Face of Jesus

A woman of courage steps forward to do what

no one else dared to do. She wipes away the blood and spittle from his face, and receives in return a precious representation of his features.

Veronica teaches us a priceless lesson: Like her, we must have the fortitude to stand with those who are friendless even though others lack the courage to draw near. At times we must even take a controversial stand which makes us look ridiculous to some.

Prayer

Lord, I praise and thank you for the Veronicas of this world. Help me to speak out on behalf of those who have no voice, even when human respect tempts me to be a coward.

Our Father. Hail Mary. Glory.

Seventh Station: Jesus Falls the Second Time

The journey is long, the burden heavy. Once more Jesus falls to the ground and lies there until he is pulled roughly to his feet again.

How difficult to get up when we are down! How difficult to rise up when we are on the bottom rung of the ladder and those above us are anxious to keep us there! Nowadays this is the situation with many minority groups who have little chance to improve their lot.

Prayer

Lord, I also need to rise up at times. I find myself afflicted with feelings of uselessness, and life seems devoid of meaning. And even though there are many important persons in my life I still feel quite lonely at times. Help me to rise up . . . and to do what I can for those who are far worse off than I.

Our Father. Hail Mary. Glory.

Eighth Station: Jesus Speaks to the Weeping Women

Women along the way weep over his bloody appearance and Jesus, a dying man, is called on to console them! He warns them to weep not for him but for their children.

As Christians we are called to have compassion toward those who are abandoned, the "losers" of this world. And we are asked to express this compassion not simply by tears but by sharing from our abundance of food, riches and talents.

Prayer

Lord, at times I feel people pressing in on me with demands. They demand my time, attention, money. Sometimes they are those I know; at other times they are those from across the world whose faces I will never see. Help me to respond to their needs as well as I

can, but remember, Lord, that my own needs
are also great.

Our Father. Hail Mary. Glory.

Ninth Station: Jesus Falls the Third Time

Weariness and suffering take their toll. Jesus
falls flat again. Once more he is dragged to his
feet, and plods on toward Calvary.

Weariness. Weariness is the alcoholic who
stumbles just when he thinks he has solved
the problem. Weariness is the depressed
woman who feels completely abandoned by
family, friends and God. Weariness is the
scrupulous person who feels plunged into the
depths of sin over a trifle. The name of the
battle is weariness.

Prayer

Lord, I know something about that weariness.
I recognize the symptoms when a relationship
goes sour and someone I love fails to return
that love. I feel that weariness when my own
mediocrity settles around me once more like a
blanket. Pick me up, Lord, and keep me going.

Our Father. Hail Mary. Glory.

Tenth Station: Jesus Is Stripped of His Garments

A poor man at birth and during his life, Jesus is poorest of all at the time of his death. Even the clothes he wears are stripped from his bleeding body.

Poverty is a way of life for millions who grub out a bare existence. Survival is all they can hope for, and sometimes even that hope vanishes. Two thousand years after Calvary, the poor are still stripped of the little they have. Am I trying to help them?

Prayer

Lord, I have more than my share of the world's goods. I find it very difficult to slake my thirst for more belongings, much less give up anything I've already accumulated. But it's not only a matter of goods. I have also been given time and talents. Help me to share what I have with those around me who need them.

Our Father. Hail Mary. Glory.

Eleventh Station: Jesus Is Nailed to the Cross

The soldiers shove Jesus onto the cross and pound nails into his hands and feet.

We cannot understand such brutality, such torture. Yet we can be tolerant of brutality which occurs in our society. For example, consider the outrages which sometimes occur in crowded jails and prisons. Can we see the difference between just punishment for offenders, and treatment which is scarcely more humane than driving nails into their limbs?

Prayer

Lord, I have my share of nails, too. A nail is an unexpected hurt, a breakdown in communication with a member of my family. It's a lost opportunity that will never come again, a would-be success that eludes my grasp at the last possible moment. Please help me bear the pain of nails like these.

Our Father. Hail Mary. Glory.

Twelfth Station: Jesus Dies on the Cross

At last the suffering is over. Jesus commits himself into his Father's hands, bows his head, and dies.

Another victim of violence. How many other innocent persons have joined him since then? His was a message of peace but we are unable to hear it over the din of battle and the shouts of those at enmity with one another. When will we ever learn?

Prayer

Lord, I find the seeds of destruction within myself. Prejudice and ill-will are not strangers to me and my tongue can slice a neighbor in two and commit "tiny murders" of its own. But you died to free me from this kind of tyranny, and I know you will help me be a messenger of your peace.

Our Father. Hail Mary. Glory.

Thirteenth Station: Jesus Is Taken Down from the Cross

Friends come forward to claim the body of Jesus. Tenderly they take him down from the cross and place him in the arms of his mother.

To the friends of Jesus the darkness of that moment must have seemed unconquerable. Likewise, the complex problems facing us can sometimes seem insurmountable. By her complete faith and trust at this time, Mary points out a way through the darkness to light.

Prayer

Lord, I am tempted at times to be discouraged by the events of my life and the problems besetting society. Please lighten the darkness of such moments and grant me a small measure of Mary's trust and faith.

Our Father. Hail Mary. Glory.

Fourteenth Station: The Burial of Jesus

His friends and relatives carry the body of Jesus to the tomb. They roll a boulder across the entrance, and withdraw in sorrow.

It looks like the end to a sad story, but we know it's only the beginning. Similarly, the suffering and desolation around us are not the final verdict on our hopes. The good news is that we are living in a universe that has been redeemed. Pain and ugliness will never win out.

Prayer

Lord, help me to bring about the day of your coming by the way I lead my life. Bury my selfishness in the tomb and grant me a stronger love for those who are close to me, and those I will never know in this life.

Our Father. Hail Mary. Glory.

Epilogue: The Resurrection

The friends and relatives of Jesus learn the incredible good news: Jesus has risen from the dead; he has overcome death.

The Way of the Cross spotlights the dark side of mankind and the dark side of ourselves. But thanks to the Resurrection there can be no despair. All suffering and pain (our own and others) becomes worthwhile and begins to make sense. We are redeemed!

Prayer

Lord, your resurrection reminds us that our lives are supremely worthwhile and that our "worthwhileness" is measured by the way we love one another. Help me to use the talents and gifts you have given me in your service and in the service of my neighbor.

Our Father. Hail Mary. Glory.

A person of prayer will do more in a year's
apostolate than another in a lifetime.
Louis Lallemant

11. The Rosary of the Blessed Virgin Mary

THE ROSARY COMBINES vocal prayer and meditation in a simple way suitable to all classes of Christians. Its 15 mysteries are arranged in groups of five, following the sequence of the life of Jesus and that of his blessed mother. Each decade of the Rosary is composed of one Our Father, 10 Hail Marys, and one Glory. Many people find that adding a suitable phrase to the first half of the Hail Mary each time helps them concentrate their attention on the mystery to be contemplated. The constant repetition of the same vocal prayers, the use of the beads themselves and the pattern of salutation and response set up a rhythm favorable to peaceful, recollected prayer. In origin the Rosary was a form of private and personal devotion and it's probably still best used in the peace and quiet of solo recitation. Sitting is normally the posture most favorable to the recollection which the Rosary fosters.

The Joyful Mysteries

1. The Angel Gabriel's Message to Mary

The Lord himself will give you a sign: A young woman shall conceive and bear a son and call his name Immanuel. Isaiah 7:15

Hail, Mary, . . . and blessed is the fruit of your womb, Jesus,

who was conceived at the message of an angel.

2. Mary's Visit to her Cousin Elizabeth

The word of the Lord came to me: "Before I formed you in the womb I knew you, and before you were born I consecrated you, a prophet to the nations I appointed you." Jeremiah 1:5

Hail, Mary, . . . the fruit of your womb, Jesus,

who consecrated the Baptist in the womb of his mother.

3. Jesus' Birth in Bethlehem of Judah

I bring you good news of great joy, joy for all the people: Today in the city of David a Savior has been born for you; he is Christ the Lord. Luke 2:11–12

Hail, Mary, . . . the fruit of your womb, Jesus,

who was born for us in the stable of Bethlehem.

4. Jesus Is Presented in the Temple

My own eyes have seen the salvation
which you have prepared in the sight of
every people: a light to reveal you to the
nations and the glory of your people Israel.
Luke 2:30–32

Hail, Mary, ... the fruit of your womb,
Jesus,

the light of the nations and the glory of
your people Israel.

5. The Boy Jesus in the Temple

Jesus said to his parents: "Why did you
have to look for me? Didn't you know that I
had to be in my Father's house? ... His
mother treasured all these things in her
heart. Luke 2:49, 51

Hail, Mary, ... the fruit of your womb,
Jesus,

the power and the wisdom of God.

Mary, our Queen, Mother of mercy,
  you are our life, our joy, our hope.
In our exile from Eden
  we turn to you as our advocate.
Look on us with eyes of pity,
  gentle and loving Mother.
Lead us home at last
  into the presence of Jesus.
Blessed is the fruit of your womb,
  Mary ever-Virgin.   *Salve Regina*

V. Pray for us, O holy Mother of God,
R. That we may be made worthy of the
    promises of Christ.

Let us pray.

Father,
in your plan for our salvation
your Word became man,
announced by an angel and born of the
    Virgin Mary.
May we who believe that she is the mother of
    God
receive the help of her prayers.
We ask this through Christ our Lord.
—Amen.

The Sorrowful Mysteries

1. The Agony of Jesus in the Garden of Gethsemane

Jesus threw himself on the ground and prayed that, if possible, he might not have to go through that time of suffering. "Abba, dear Father, all things are possible for you. Take this cup of suffering from me. Yet not what I want, but what you want." Mark 14:35–36

Hail, Mary, ... the fruit of your womb Jesus,

who was offered up because he willed it.

2. The Scourging of Jesus at the Pillar

Pilate wanted to please the crowd, so he set Barabbas free for them. Then he had Jesus whipped and handed him over to be crucified. Mark 15:15

Hail, Mary, ... the fruit of your womb, Jesus,

who was bruised for our offenses.

3. The Crowning of Jesus with Thorns

The soldiers made a crown out of thorny branches and put it on his head; then they put a purple robe on him and came to him and said, "Long live the King of the Jews!" And they went up and slapped him. John 19:2–3

Hail, Mary, . . . the fruit of your womb, Jesus,
a man of sorrows and acquainted with grief.

4. Jesus Walks the Way of the Cross

Pilate handed Jesus over to them to be crucified. So they took charge of Jesus. He went out, carrying his cross, and came to "The Place of the Skull," as it is called. Two other men, both of them criminals, were also led out to be put to death with Jesus. John 19:16–17; Luke 23:32
Hail, Mary, . . . the fruit of your womb, Jesus,
who was crushed for our sins.

5. Jesus is Crucified and Dies on the Cross

It was about 12 o'clock when the sun stopped shining, and darkness covered the whole country until three o'clock; the curtain hanging in the Temple was torn in two. Jesus cried out in a loud voice, "Father, in your hands I place my spirit!" He said this and died. John 23: 44–46
Hail, Mary, . . . the fruit of your womb, Jesus,
by whose wounds we are healed.

After the Sorrowful Mysteries:

We turn to you for protection,
   holy Mother of God.
From your place in heaven
   help us in all our needs.
Blessed Virgin in glory,
   save us from every danger.
                    Sub Tuum Praesidium

V. Mother of Sorrows, pray for us,
R. That we may be made worthy of the
   promises of Christ.

Let us pray.

Father,
as your Son was raised on the cross,
his mother Mary stood by him, sharing his
      sufferings.
May your Church be united with Christ
in his suffering and death
and so come to share in his rising to new life,
where he lives and reigns with you and the
      Holy Spirit,
one God, for ever and ever.
—Amen.

The Glorious Mysteries

1. Christ Rises from the Grave

The Messiah had to suffer and rise from the dead three days later, and in his name the need of a change of heart and the forgiveness of sins must be preached to all nations. Luke 24:46–47

Hail, Mary, ... the fruit of your womb, Jesus,

who died for our sins and rose for our justification.

2. Christ Ascends into Heaven

After the Lord Jesus had talked with them, he was taken up to heaven and sat at the right hand of God. His disciples went and preached everywhere and the Lord worked with them and confirmed their message. Mark 16:19–20

Hail, Mary, ... the fruit of your womb, Jesus,

who now sits at the right hand of the Father.

3. The Gift of the Holy Spirit

When the Holy Spirit comes upon you, you will be filled with power and you will be witnesses for me to the ends of the earth. Acts 1:8

Hail, Mary,... the fruit of your womb, Jesus,
who sends us the Holy Spirit as he promised.

4. The Falling Asleep and Assumption of Our Lady

What is mortal must be changed into what is immortal; what will die must be changed into what cannot die. Thanks be to God who gives us the victory through our Lord Jesus Christ. 1 Corinthians 15:53, 57
Hail, Mary,... the fruit of your womb, Jesus,
who makes all things new.

5. The Coronation of Our Lady and the Glory of all the Saints

A great sign appeared in the sky: a woman clothed with the sun, with the moon under her feet, and on her head a crown of 12 stars. She gave birth to a Son who was to rule all nations with a rod of iron. Revelation 12:1, 5
Hail, Mary,... the fruit of your womb, Jesus,
who will come again in glory to judge the living and the dead.

After the Glorious Mysteries:

Joy fill your heart, O Queen most high,
    alleluia!
  Your Son who in the tomb did lie, alleluia!
Has risen as he did prophesy, alleluia!
    Pray for us, Mother, when we die, alleluia!
                                    Regina Coeli

V. Rejoice and be glad, O Virgin Mary,
    alleluia,
R. For the Lord has truly risen, alleluia.

Let us pray.

God our Father,
you give joy to the world
by the resurrection of your Son, our Lord
    Jesus Christ.
Through the prayers of his mother, the
    Virgin Mary,
bring us to the happiness of eternal life.
We ask this through Christ our Lord.
—Amen.

Nothing is more powerful than prayer.
    Indeed nothing is comparable to it.
                            St. John Chrysostom

12. The Message We Proclaim

In His Infinite Goodness

In his infinite goodness,   *(Eph 2:7)*
the Father in heaven has called us   *(I Pt 5:10)*
to be united with him in life and joy, *(Jn 17:21)*
sharing his divine riches: *(Eph 2:7)*

through Christ, his Son—   *(I Pt 5:10)*
him he gave as a ransom for us sinners,
              (I Tim 2:6; I Jn 4:10)
and into his likeness he desires that we be
    conformed,   *(Rm 8:29)*

so that, born anew of water and the Holy
    Spirit,   *(Jn 3:5)*
and thus made partakers of the divine
    nature,   *(I Pt 1:4)*
we may be children of God.   *(I Jn 3:1)*

And because we are God's children,
he has sent the Spirit of his Son into our
      hearts: *(Gal 4:6)*

thus being the temple of God *(I Cor 6:19)*
we are to live the life of God's children,
                       (Rm 6:4)
following the example of Christ, our firstborn
      brother, *(Rm 8:29)*

so that we may gain the kingdom of God and
      his glory, as heirs of God, *(I Th 2:12)*
joint heirs with Christ. *(Rm 8:17)*

Johannes Hofinger, S.J.

Jesus Christ Is Lord

Christ always had the very nature of God
  but he did not think that by force
he should try to become equal with God.
Instead of this, of his own free will he gave it
    all up,
  and took the nature of a servant.
He became like man
  and appeared in human likeness.
He was humble and walked the path of
    obedience
all the way to death—
  his death on the cross.

For this reason God raised him
to the highest place above
  and gave him the name
that is greater than any other name.
And so, in honor of the name of Jesus,
all beings in heaven, on earth
and in the world below
  will fall on their knees,
and all will openly proclaim that
  Jesus Christ is Lord,
    to the glory of God the Father.

Phil 2:6–11

Christ, the Son

Christ is the visible likeness of the invisible
    God.
He is the firstborn Son, superior to all created
    things.
For through him God created everything in
    heaven and on the earth,
  the seen and the unseen things, including
    spiritual powers, lords, rulers and
    authorities.
God created the whole universe through him
    and for him.
He existed before all things, and in union
    with him all things have their proper
    place.

Christ is the Head of his body, the Church;
  he is the source of the body's life.

He is the firstborn Son, who was raised from
    death,
  in order that he alone might have the first
    place in all things.
For it was by God's own decision
  that the Son has in himself the full nature
    of God.
Through the Son, then, God decided to bring
    the whole universe back to himself.
God made peace through his Son's death on
    the cross,
  and so brought back to himself all things,
  both on earth and in heaven.

Col 1:15–20

God's Plan of Salvation

Let us give thanks to the God and Father
of our Lord Jesus Christ!
For in our union with Christ he has blessed
us
by giving us every spiritual blessing
in the heavenly world.
Even before the world was made,
God had already chosen us to be his
through our union with Christ,
so that we would be holy and without fault
before him.

Because of his love God had already decided
that through Jesus Christ he would make
us his sons—
this was his pleasure and purpose.
Let us praise God for his glorious grace,
for the free gift he gave us in his dear Son!

For by the death of Christ we are set free,
that is, our sins are forgiven.
How great is the grace of God, which he
gave us in such large measure!

In all his wisdom and insight God did what
he had purposed,
and made known to us the secret plan
he had already decided to complete
by means of Christ.
This plan, which God will complete when the
time is right,

is to bring all creation together, everything
   in heaven and on earth, with Christ as
   head.

All things are done according to God's plan
      and decision;
And God chose us to be his own people in
      union with Christ
   because of his own purpose,
based on what he had decided from the very
      beginning.
Let us, then, who were the first to hope in
      Christ,
praise God's glory!

And you also became God's people
   when you heard the true message,
   the Good News that brought you salvation.
You believed in Christ,
   and God has put his stamp of ownership
      on you
by giving you the Holy Spirit he had
      promised.
The Spirit is the guarantee
   that we shall receive what God has
      promised his people,
   and this assures us that God will give
      complete freedom
   to those who are his.
Let us praise his glory!

Eph 1:3–14

The Great Mystery

No one can deny how great is the secret of
    our religion:

Christ appeared in human form,
    was shown to be right by the Spirit,
    and was seen by angels.
He was preached among the nations,
    was believed in throughout the world,
    and was taken up to heaven.

At the right time, he will be revealed by God,
    the blessed and only Ruler of all,
The King of kings and the Lord of lords.
    He alone is immortal.

To him be honor and eternal power! Amen.

1 Tim 3:16; 6:15–16

Holy, Holy, Holy

Holy, holy, holy is the Lord
    God Almighty,
Who was, who is, and who is
    to come.

Our Lord and our God! You are worthy
    to receive glory, honor, and power.
For you created all things,
    and by your will they were given existence
    and life.

Rv 4:8, 11

Worthy Is the Lamb

You are worthy to take the scroll
   and to break open its seals.
For you were killed,
   and by your death you bought people for
      God
  of every tribe, race, language and nation.
You made them a kingdom of priests
    to serve our God
and they shall rule on earth.

The lamb who was killed is worthy
to receive power, wealth, wisdom, strength,
  honor, glory and praise!

To him who sits on the throne and to the
    Lamb,
be all praise and honor, glory and might.
   Forever and ever!

Rv 5:9–10, 12, 13

The glory of God is a human being who is
    fully alive, and the life of such a person
    consists in beholding God.

St. Irenaeus of Lyons

Psalm 150   Universal Praise

Alleluia!
Praise God in his holy place.
 Praise him in the heaven of his power.
Praise him for his mighty deeds.
 Praise him for his excelling greatness.
Praise him with the blast of the horn.
 Praise him with harp and lyre.
Praise him with drum and dance.
 Praise him with strings and pipe.
Praise him with resounding cymbals.
 Praise him with clashing cymbals.
Let everything with breath
 praise the Lord.
Alleluia!

Acknowledgments

Community of St. Mary the Virgin, Wantage, England. For "For Perfect Love."

Concordia Publishing House. *Psalms/Now* by Leslie F. Brandt. © 1973. For "Now That I Have Found You" (Paraphrase on Psalm 63).

E. J. Dwyer Publishers. *The Pope's Family Prayer Book.* © 1976. For "A Prayer for Husbands and Wives," "For Our Children," "For the Sick," "For the Aged," and "For Civil Authorities."

Farrar, Straus & Giroux, Inc. *Thoughts in Solitude* by Thomas Merton. © 1956, 1958 by the Abbey of Our Lady of Gethsemani. For "The Road Ahead." Reprinted with the permission of Farrar, Straus & Giroux, Inc.

Fortress Press. *Campus Prayers for the '70s* by John W. Vannorsdall. © 1970. For "For Parents in Trouble."

Franciscan Herald Press. *Writings of St. Francis of Assisi*, ed. Benen Fahy, O.F.M. © 1964. For "Salutation to the Blessed Virgin Mary."

Charles M. Guilbert, Custodian. *Prayers, Thanksgivings and Litanies.* © 1973. For "For the Church," "For Families," and "Prayer to the Holy Spirit."

List of Prayers, Psalms, Canticles...

365